W. J Hocking

Modern Problems and Christian Ethics

W. J Hocking

Modern Problems and Christian Ethics

ISBN/EAN: 9783337026806

Printed in Europe, USA, Canada, Australia, Japan

Cover: Foto ©Lupo / pixelio.de

More available books at **www.hansebooks.com**

MODERN PROBLEMS

AND

CHRISTIAN ETHICS.

BY

W. J. HOCKING,

Vicar of All Saints', Tufnell Park, N.,

AUTHOR OF
'MORS JANUA VITÆ,' 'THREE HOURS AT THE CROSS,' ETC.

'Je me contente de ce qui peut s'écrire, et je rêve tout ce qui peut se rêver.'
DE SÉVIGNÉ.

LONDON:
WELLS GARDNER, DARTON & CO.,
3, PATERNOSTER BUILDINGS, E.C.
AND 44, VICTORIA STREET, S.W.

DEDICATION.

To the Congregation worshipping in All Saints' Parish Church, Tufnell Park, N., who heard these sermons, and at whose urgent request I now give them to the world, I dedicate them in this permanent form with sincere affection and regard.

W. J. H.

PREFACE.

I HAVE consented to the publication of these twelve Sermons not because I am conscious that their literary merit will commend them to the world, nor because they contain anything very new, striking, or original, but mainly because those who heard them have repeatedly expressed a wish to have them in a permanent form.

That, as literary efforts, they are very faulty no critic will say with more assurance than I do; but the love which prompted the wish to have them as they are will forgive the many faults in print, as it forgave the many faults in preaching.

One thing only I claim for them, and that is that they are an earnest attempt to meet the many difficulties which are troubling the minds of the very best of our young men and women. If they help one soul to higher ideals of life and conduct, then I shall have the only reward I desire.

They were preached at intervals on the first Sunday evening in the month—when it is my rule to deal with 'popular' topics. As some of the intervals were long, that

PREFACE

must be my apology for occasional repetitions of thought and expression. They contain many thoughts which, doubtless, at the time of preparation were borrowed from various sources, too numerous to mention here even if I could remember them; and to crowd the pages with footnotes of references would not be a source of either interest or profit to the ordinary reader. The sermons are addressed to 'the man in the street,' and not to the scholar or the critic.

Some of them were reported at the time of preaching in religious journals, both in England and America. The sermon on 'Amusements' was published in a volume of sermons edited by the Rev. Prebendary Kitto, and entitled 'Religion in Common Life.' My thanks are due to him for allowing me to reprint it. The one on 'The Animal World' was published as a pamphlet by the Society for Promoting Kindness to Animals, and dedicated to her Grace the Duchess of Portland; but as the edition of that pamphlet (five thousand) is now exhausted, I include the sermon here by request.

W. J. HOCKING.

JANUARY, 1898.

CONTENTS.

	PAGE
AMUSEMENTS IN THE LIGHT OF CHRISTIAN ETHICS	1
THE THEATRE IN THE LIGHT OF CHRISTIAN ETHICS	15
POLITICS IN THE LIGHT OF CHRISTIAN ETHICS	33
SOCIETY'S WASTES IN THE LIGHT OF CHRISTIAN ETHICS	49
WAR IN THE LIGHT OF CHRISTIAN ETHICS	65
GAMBLING IN THE LIGHT OF CHRISTIAN ETHICS	79
LONDON PROBLEMS IN THE LIGHT OF CHRISTIAN ETHICS	93
LABOUR PROBLEMS IN THE LIGHT OF CHRISTIAN ETHICS	105
THE SUNDAY QUESTION IN THE LIGHT OF CHRISTIAN ETHICS	121
PARENTAL DUTIES IN THE LIGHT OF CHRISTIAN ETHICS	135
THE ANIMAL WORLD IN THE LIGHT OF CHRISTIAN ETHICS	151
FOOLS!	165

1 CORINTHIANS x. 31.

'Whether therefore ye eat, or drink, or whatsoever ye do, do all to the glory of God.'

AMUSEMENTS

IN THE LIGHT OF CHRISTIAN ETHICS.

NOTHING in connection with our holy religion is more difficult to realize than that this and kindred maxims are as binding on us as on the people to whom they were primarily addressed. We have somehow got into the way of thinking that the blessings of Christianity are for us, but that its rules of life, as inculcated in the New Testament, were for the early Christians, the believers of long ago. Do we not, when we read of giving up to Redeeming Love, of bearing the daily cross, of presenting body and soul a living sacrifice, of being so possessed of God as to be His Temple—do we not imagine that these words are not for us? They are histories of appeals, the records of inculcations, the accounts of demands made on the peoples of a far-away past—the early disciples, the first martyrs, the Christians who immediately succeeded the Christ.

We err: the principles of Christianity, the ethics of Christianity, the spirit of Christianity, the claims of Christianity, are ever the same—for all time and for all peoples. They can never be obsolete, never be referred to some far-distant past; they are for one long eternal PRESENT, the infinite NOW, the everlasting TO-DAY.

It is here that men make such grievous mistakes, when they talk of Christianity as out of date, as played out, fossilized in the strata of history. If it were a theological system, or a code of rules, or a stereotyped creed, or a string of pious platitudes, it might become out of date; but it is *spirit*, life, force, principle, passion, that may for ever be appropriated by the living ego, and ever inspire the beating heart of man. For humanity are its ethics, for all time its principles, for eternity its inspiring power. Tell me of one of its cardinal principles that is behind the age; one of its essential maxims that is without application to modern life and modern conditions, and I will seek some new religion. The fault is, not that Christianity is played out, but that men's determination to live it is played out; not that its ethics are out of date, but that men do not rise to them; not that its maxims are behind the time, but that they are so far in front that men's aspirations do not reach them.

They are still primal principles

'That shine aloft like stars.'

One thing, however, that we shall do well to remember is, that these principles have a general, and not a particular, application; I mean by that, that they do not apply so much to details as to the governing motives of life. If you search the Bible through you will find no list of duties, of pleasures, of contingencies to which its ethics, its maxims, its principles may be applied. Why? Not because it is not adaptable to all, but because it is a spirit, a temper, a quality, a ruling principle, intended to pervade everything, inspire everything, transfuse everything, rather than a code of rules which may be nailed against the many doors of our life's outgoings and incomings. It has nothing to say of the different callings in which men are engaged; nothing to say of dignities or menialities as applied to duties. It lays down no law as to callings which are compatible with high ideals and heavenly aspirations. It does not distinguish between the different trades and occupations and engagements which are helpful and those which are harmful. It comes in no narrow, dictatorial spirit to men, saying, 'Thou shalt do this,' and 'Thou shalt not do that.' All this it leaves to the individual conscience and to the sanctified common sense of men. But it insists on this: 'Whatsoever ye do, do all to the glory of God.' That is the determining principle by which all actions must be judged, and approved or condemned.

Hence it comes that amusements, as such, have no place in the ethical teachings of the New Testament. Not because they would be out of place there, but because they must be subject, with all the other phases of life, to the primary principle.

And yet men have often made the mistake of supposing that because the New Testament, and the Bible generally, is silent on the question of amusements, it therefore discountenances, and by that very fact condemns, amusements. No fallacy could be more stupid or more mischievous than that. It were just as wise, just as sensible, just as reasonable, to say that because the many phases of domestic and commercial life are not mentioned in the New Testament, therefore those phases of life are unchristian.

The New Testament says nothing about personal cleanliness; does anyone conclude from that that it is unchristian to be clean? The New Testament is not concerned with personal habits, personal tastes, personal exercises; it is only careful to say that all these things must be brought into conformity with God's will; that all must be done as under His eye, and unto His glory. It is an abominable, a blasphemous, and a wicked wrong to teach that whatever is not prescribed for in the New Testament is outside Christianity, and a thing with which a Christian has no concern.

A fact that must be recognised is that amusements in some form are necessaries of life. I do not say essential to living, but certainly essential to the right development of all our faculties, the right enjoyment of life's many and varied scenes, the right performance of life's duties. There is, therefore, nothing undignified, unmanly, unheroic, unchristian, in amusing and in being amused. Everything that is pure is compatible with 'perfecting holiness in the fear of God.'

What is the grand ideal of the New Testament so far as our psychical and physical natures are concerned? Is it not expressed in the old Roman motto: '*Mens sana in corpore sano*'? Yes; the body that, according to St. Paul, was meant to be the temple of the Holy Ghost, the temple of God, must be kept healthy as well as holy; in perfect soundness as well as in perfect purity. In fact, healthiness is a part of holiness, soundness is an essential of purity.

Let me, then, try to give you some practical hints as to the bearing of Christian ethics upon this vital question.

(*a*) Christianity certainly teaches that amusement is not the end and aim of life.

Upon all alike—every man and woman born into the world—it lays the abiding obligation of work. It tells us plainly that idleness is the negation of the Divine Law, and that in honest useful work lies the fulfilment of the Divine purpose. The Master Himself not only sanctified toil, but made it an essential condition of participating in the heavenly kingdom. He spoke of His Heavenly Father as working from all eternity, and of His own determination to follow His Father's example: 'My Father worketh hitherto, and I work'; 'I must work the works of Him that sent Me while it is day.' And every commission given to His disciples, every exhortation, every maxim, every moral principle, implies a life of activity. The results of idleness, inanity, indifference to duty, He sets forth with terrific power in parable and simile, in sermon and wayside speech.

His Apostles occupy the same ground: 'If a man will not work, neither let him eat,' says St. Paul. 'Quit you like men, be strong,' is his charge to the Corinthians. Of the vagrant parasite he says: 'If any provide not for his own, and specially for those of his own house, he hath denied the faith, and is worse than an infidel.'

It is therefore perfectly plain what the intention of Christianity is as to the main aim and end of life. Everything must be subordinate to the fulfilling of duty in that sphere of life to which it has pleased God to call us. Here, then, we are clear: we tread unmistakable ground—a man must not work in order that he may find means and opportunity for amusement, but he must have amusement that he may be the better fitted to work. Duty is the end of life, pleasure a means to that end.

Is there not a tendency to look upon toil, labour, occupation as a something essential because of what it will procure us, rather than as the great purpose of God in us? And do not men work, when they work at all, with an eye to the pleasures which the results of their labour will bring them? There are men and women with whom amusement is the only pursuit, as though the world were a garden planted and tended by angel-visitants, and as though the end of human life consisted in sucking the sweetness out of its flowers. How many men are there with no other thought than that of enjoyment—enjoyment of the senses, of the passions, of the appetites! How many women with no greater concern than to dance at the next ball, to flirt at the next party, to see the next play, to read the next novel, to long for the next season!

Great God in heaven! and is it for this that Thou didst make man in Thine own image: for this that Thou didst endow him with wisdom, insight, knowledge, reason, skill? Has Thy purpose in woman been fulfilled in these low aims? Is there nothing higher for man than to be a constant digester of rich food? nothing nobler for woman than to be a walking illustration of the latest fashion?

In a world full of activities, full of intricate economies, throbbing with interests that reach out to every hand capable of work, and to every mind capable of thought, who dares fritter away life in a whirl of sportive pleasure? Go forth to your lawful amusements, but make them subservient to noble deeds. It is by thus doing your duty that you will be able to extract the honey out of the world's sweetness; by the consecration of holy deeds to holy ends that you will have time to hear the music which the finger of God evolves as He sweeps the chords of the universe.

(*b*) Another principle found in the ethics of Christianity is that of judicious discernment through an enlightened understanding and an educated conscience.

It states that things which may be perfectly lawful are not always expedient; it declares that while 'to the pure all things are pure,' circumstances and influences have to be weighed in their relation to others; it makes much of that solidarity of interest which underlies man's relationship with man; and, above all, it places man's kinship with God as the potent determining power between the right and the wrong, the helpful and the harmful. Here, then, we have a law for our guidance. It does not follow that, because amusement is lawful and good, everything that amuses is lawful and good. Its influence upon ourselves, upon our brother, upon society, upon the world at large, and upon posterity has to be taken into the count.

These considerations at once determine the Christian against all amusements that are vicious, or that lead to vice. There may be a hundred things which would give pleasure to the senses, the passions, the appetites, but against which reason and conscience, law social, law moral, and law Divine enter an edict: these, of course, the Christian man abstains from. A man might find such pleasure in a free use of the intoxicating cup as to lose his reason, lose his self-respect, lose his love of home, lose the nobler features of his manhood, and degrade himself down to a level with the brute; but Christian principle, the spirit of

Christ in him, restrains him: he hears an inner voice saying, 'Your bodies are the temples of the Holy Ghost. . . . Glorify God in your bodies.' And if he heeds not that voice he is not a Christian.

And what is true of drunkenness is true also of other forms of vice: things that may be pleasurable, that may afford abundant *amusement*—in the original meaning of that word—are yet forbidden to the Christian because they are alien to that high purpose of life which God has revealed to us in His Son, in our conscience and our reason. Heed not the sublime ethics of the New Testament, turn a deaf ear to the heavenly voices that cry from the lofty peaks of holiness—'Keep thyself pure,' stifle the inner voice of conscience—which is the voice of God—and you may have amusement, but you will be like a ship with all her sails spread to the wind, and with no ballast to steady her, and no helm to guide her, and sooner or later must inevitably be sucked into the whirlpool of destruction, or driven on to the beetling rocks of ruin.

There are many of our young people giving themselves up to things which, no doubt, are pleasurable from an animal point of view, but yet things which are forming in them habits which will be like a millstone around their neck till they finally sink in the maelstrom of perdition. There are others outwardly religious; men and women whose baby-brows were marked with the sign of the cross; who in youth voluntarily took it upon themselves to keep God's holy will and commandments, and walk in the same all the days of their life; who, perchance, have knelt at the altar of Sacramental grace and benediction, who yet are fostering and indulging habits which the hallowed surroundings of this sacred place forbid me to mention. Where, oh, where is their Christianity? Where is the Spirit of Christ that should rule them? They are simply de-Christianizing themselves by their follies; bolting the door of the heavenly kingdom against themselves which no human hand can unlock, and which perchance angels and God Himself may be unable to open. There are some things which even the Eternal cannot do; one of these is the undoing of the consequences of wrong. If men persist in pursuing evil He cannot but let them reap the fruit of their doings.

It is the business of the Christian on earth to flee that which is evil, and to follow that which is good; to prove all things, and to hold fast only that which is pure, and lovely, and of good report. God will help you to do it if you ask Him, the example of Christ will help you, the indwelling spirit of Him 'Who did no sin, neither was guile found in His mouth,' will help you. Take heed that something helps you to that which is good; take heed that something keeps you from that which is evil. Pray more and more for the spirit of discernment, and of sound knowledge.

You, perhaps, will expect that I should give you a catalogue of the things which Christianity approves, and that I should warn you against those things that Christianity disapproves. I have already done the latter—in spirit, at least. It is in the power of no human being to do the former. I am no modern Moses; to no man to-day is it given to say, 'Thou shalt do this,' and 'Thou shalt not do that.' What may be perfectly right for one man may be perfectly and absolutely wrong for another. 'To him who esteemeth anything to be unclean, to him it is unclean. . . . Happy is he that condemneth not himself in that thing which he alloweth.'

No rule in regard to this can ever be anything but misleading: circumstances have to be taken into account, individual character has to be taken into account, influences on others have to be taken into account. 'No man liveth unto himself, and none of us dieth unto himself.'

I can therefore only give you a few hints for your guidance, and not a code of laws for your observance. Whatever is essentially manly, essentially womanly, that certainly is Christian. Whatever amusement recreates you, soothes you, invigorates you, and tends to fit you for duty, and *leaves no sting behind it*, be assured that that is safe; on that you may ask the Divine blessing; in that you may feel you are glorifying God.

I am continually being asked if I think it right to dance, right to go to the theatre, right to play cards, right to play billiards. Who am I that I should determine these things? To me they might all be perfectly harmless. Every one of them I might enter into with zest, and be none the worse, but all the better, for it. But I will not, because I cannot, decide for you. If you are in doubt, decide the matter on your knees, and let it be a matter as between yourself and God alone.

On the other hand, I would say, Anything that gives you low motives, low aims, low desires; anything that creates lust, that arouses passion, that suggests impurity, that makes you morally weak, that dissipates your energies, or makes you a fornicator like Esau, who for one morsel of meat sold his birthright, that for you is absolutely and everlastingly wrong. Hence it comes that, while it is right for one to dance, for another it is wrong. In the thing itself there is no absolute quality: it becomes right or wrong according to the influence which it exercises on its votary. The same may be said of the theatre, of cards, of many games and sports: 'All things are lawful, but all things are not expedient' to all men. Again I quote St. Paul: 'Happy is he that condemneth not himself in that thing which he alloweth.' Where there is doubt, safety lies on the side of abstention. 'Let every man be fully persuaded in his own mind.'

The last principle which time will allow me to deal with is that which is involved in the dual nature and capacities of man.

Christianity claims attention to both sides of our natures —body and spirit. It tells us that we live two lives: one which stands related to the world that we can see; the other to the spirit world. It teaches us that the things which we can see are temporal, transitory, passing away; that the things which lie beyond the reach of the visual are abiding and for ever.

In view of this, is it not strange that most of our care is about the body and the things which pertain to it? To seek and serve the present—the gay, the giddy, the flippant, the fleeting—that is our chief concern. I know that the body has its claims, and no claims of the soul must suffer us to ignore them. I admit, as I have stated, that the claims of the body demand amusement, relaxation, recreation, exercise. I admit that these, rightly used, not only contribute to the health and purity of the body, but to the health and purity of the soul. But the body is not all of us: it is but the smallest part. This life is not all: it is the threshold of the eternal world. Why, then, give it all our care? Why not so use it, with its myriad pure pleasures, its bright and beautiful things, as I believe we may use it, as a means of preparation for the inheritance of the saints in light? But ever have before you this truth, that

> 'The worst of miseries
> Is when a nature, framed for nobler things,
> Condemns itself in life to petty joys,
> And, sore athirst for air, breathes scanty life
> Gasping from out the shallows!'

The Theatre
IN THE LIGHT OF CHRISTIAN ETHICS.

ROMANS xiv. 13, 14.

'Let us not therefore judge one another any more; but judge this rather, that no man put a stumbling-block or an occasion to fall in his brother's way. I know, and am persuaded by the Lord Jesus, that there is nothing unclean of itself; but to him that esteemeth anything to be unclean, to him it is unclean.'

THE THEATRE

IN THE LIGHT OF CHRISTIAN ETHICS.

THAT was a principle which St. Paul laid down in regard to the rightness or wrongness of eating certain meats which had been first offered in sacrifice to some heathen idol, and then sold in the shambles for food, and also in regard to certain meats which Jewish ceremonialism pronounced unclean.

The thing was not to be judged on its own inherent merit, but on the merit of its influence on those immediately affected. In the one case, he says that to eat meat which had been offered in sacrifice to an idol cannot possibly be in itself a wrong thing, because as an idol is nothing in the world but a mass of inert matter, so anything offered in sacrifice to an idol is as pure after the offering as it was before. But, on the other hand, if a man thinks that contact with an idol has made the meat impure, it is that man's duty to abstain from the meat. Believing it to be impure makes it impure to him.

Moreover, he argues, there is a light other than that of self in which the question has to be considered, that is, the solidarity of interest and responsibility which underlies Christian life. 'For none of us liveth to himself, and no man dieth to himself.' We are all members of a family, each one of which is affected by the other's conduct and character. So that a thing may in itself be perfectly harmless, and a man may use it and be perfectly innocent, so far as he himself is concerned; yet if the using of a thing puts a stumbling-block in the way of another; if it offends him, angers him, leads him to excess, or brings him into surroundings which are dangerous, then it is harmful. 'It is good,' he says, 'neither to eat flesh, nor to drink wine, nor anything whereby thy brother stumbleth or is made weak.' Our moral relationships make isolation impossible: rightness and wrongness, helpfulness and harmfulness are questions which have to be determined by reference to the community rather than the individual.

And the law which he laid down in regard to meat offered to idols he also laid down in regard to all the externals of religious and communal life. The observance or non-observance of a thing must be governed by circumstances, and by the relation of individuals, as units, to society, as an aggregate. 'To the pure all things are pure'; but there may be conditions and circumstances in which even a pure action had better be kept back because of its bearing upon others, who, on the one hand, may misinterpret it, or, on the other hand, may seek to copy it, and, from want of a clear knowledge or a well-disciplined will, stumble and fall.

That is the ethics of Christianity in regard to things doubtful, and things which are not in the abstract wrong; that is the rule which, as Christians, we are bound to apply to everything that affects communal life, that affects society, that affects our neighbour. To us it may be perfectly right, perfectly innocent, perfectly harmless, but if it is harmful to another, then to do it is wrong. The converse is equally true—the thing may be perfectly right in itself, perfectly harmless, perfectly innocent, but if the doing of it offends our conscience, if while we are doing it we feel we are doing wrong, then to us it is wrong, though another man doing the same thing may rejoice in the fact that he is doing it to the glory of God.

That is the principle which I want to apply to the subject that is to occupy our attention now. And I want to say at the very beginning that in the abstract there cannot be any possible wrong in histrionic display. Drama in itself may be as legitimate as poetry or painting, and the theatre is not necessarily more inherently evil than the concert-room. Dramatic art is very near akin to some methods employed even by the Deity Himself to unfold or teach certain aspects of Divine truth. There can be little doubt that some of the early writings of the Bible (such, for instance, as the Book of Job) were cast in the form of a dramatic poem. The love of dramatic spectacle and dramatic representation, moreover, seems to be inherent in human nature. The earliest sport of children is generally associated with the personation of some character other than that which they really are, and from the earliest dawn of civilization acting, with its various and varying arts, has appealed to the ineradicable instinct in man, young and old alike. Poetry, music, and painting have vied with each other in their splendid endeavours to adorn it; genius has devoted her sublimest efforts to the ennobling of it; philosophy has stooped from her high throne to direct its musings and to shape its characters, and religion itself—heathen and Christian alike—has approved and blest it.

Perhaps, therefore, I can best deal with the subject if I first give you a brief sketch of the history of the drama in connection with histrionic art.

Whatever may have been the crude forms that the drama took in prehistoric times, there is little doubt that the theatre, as it at present exists, arose in Greece, 'that wonderful country whose days of glory have left such a never-dying blaze of radiance behind them.' At first it seems to have taken the form of a kind of fantastic orgy of shepherds and peasants, who solemnized the rites of Bacchus by the sacrifice of a goat, by tumultuous dances, and by a sort of masquerade, in which the songs and jests corresponded in coarseness to the character of the satyrs and fawns which they were supposed to assume in honour of their patron. Out of this rude, crude, and vulgar form of entertainment, Thespis, aided by one Susarion, is said to have been the first to organize a display on a stage. And from the moment that he rescued it from barbarism it began to move with rapid strides towards an ideal perfection. Upon Æschylus, one of the Athenian generals in the battle of Marathon, B.C. 490, Greece conferred the title of the 'Father of Tragedy.' He was the first who, availing himself of Thespis's invention of the stage, introduced a number of actors upon the boards at the same time, and converted into action and dialogue the dull monologue of the Thespian orator. It was he who invented the deceptions of stage scenery, and the relief of orchestral music varied by accompanying choruses. It was he who at

Athens built the first theatre, and surrounded the drama with the embellishments of Grecian art; he who first introduced machinery for the ascent of phantoms, the descent of deities and other spectacular effects, which were as common in the Grecian theatre as in the modern English one. Under him Athens, the most learned and most highly-civilized city of the ancient world, became wholly fascinated with the splendours of this new form of entertainment. It was for her stage that Sophocles and Euripides wrote their immortal dramas, and from her libraries of dramatic poems that we have received thoughts that breathe with the loftiest ideals, and words that burn with the noblest conceptions of life. St. Paul himself did not disdain to quote to an Athenian audience a passage from the Greek poet Aratus.

We come next to Rome. Until the contact of Grecian with Roman civilization, there is little evidence that Rome had anything approaching a regular and recognised drama. They were not without a sort of rude form of dramatic entertainment, but it took the form of crude satirical farce, and was both without beauty, and utterly devoid of literary or histrionic merit. With the influx of Grecian art came the gorgeousness of the Grecian stage. Livius Andronicus is accredited with the work of transplanting the theatre from Athens to Rome, where it flourished under the immediate patronage of her successive emperors, and was supported by the best talent of her greatest writers. So popular had the stage become in the time of Nero, that he commanded all the theatres to be covered with gold. 'Some of the buildings were so large that they enclosed trees and statues, fountains and streamlets. In order to cool and refresh the multitudes assembled to witness the play, a mixture of water, wine and Sicilian saffron was prepared, and led through pipes to the highest seats, and from thence it distilled in fine rain that purified and cooled the air throughout the building.' One theatre (that of Marcus Æmilius Scaurus) was large enough to accommodate eighty thousand people. There is little doubt, too, that the theatre continued its hold upon the Romans until it was buried under the ruins of that mighty empire, to await resurrection in another form.

Where it next made its appearance is a question of dispute. Probably Rome saw the last of the stage as a secular display for at least one thousand years. When next it made its appearance it was under the guise of religion. In the Eastern Empire religious exhibitions of a theatrical character appear to have been instituted about 990 A D., by Theophylact, Patriarch of Constantinople, with the intention, as Warton surmises, of weaning the minds of the people from the Pagan revels, by substituting Christian spectacles, partaking of the same spirit of license. But history only records this as a blot on the Christianity of that age. Cedrenus tells us that 'it scandalized God and the memory of His saints.'

But a form of theatrical display, representing Christian pilgrimages, Bible scenes and stories, seems to have been common to all Christian countries in mediæval times. In France we find the pilgrims, on their return from the Holy Land, setting up a stage, and acting the scenes through which they had passed. This form of entertainment was soon followed by Scriptural plays. To make these displays more effective and imposing, a special building was erected in which there were three scaffoldings above each other, the highest so arranged as to represent heaven, the next the world, the third hell. For a time it seems to have been a purely religious form of entertainment, near akin to the modern Passion Play of Oberammergau; but it soon became associated with such debauchery and impurity that it had to be suppressed by a special enactment of the Government.

In England dramatic entertainments, representing the lives of the saints and the most eminent Scriptural stories, were known as early as the twelfth century, and were called 'miracle plays.' Chaucer tells us that in his time 'Plays of Miracles were the common resort of idle gossips in Lent.' Warton, in his 'History of English Poetry,' says 'these pieces frequently required the introduction of allegorical characters,' such as Faith, Hope, Charity, Sin, Death. But the indecencies of the thing may be gathered from the fact that Adam and Eve were personated in their primeval state of nudity in the Garden of Eden; the blasphemies of the thing from the fact that the Deity Himself was personated on the stage, and Satan and his imps were introduced to excite the mirthfulness of the audience; and the stupidity of the thing from the facts that Moses was placed on the stage arrayed in alb and cope, that David was robed in a green vestment, and that Balaam, with an immense pair of spurs, was made to ride on a wooden ass, in which was enclosed a speaker to rebuke the foolhardy prophet.

The earliest positive mention of professional actors in England, as distinct from minstrels, choristers and clergy, who chiefly participated in the miracle plays, occurs about the middle of the fifteenth century. The two earliest buildings erected in London exclusively for theatrical representation were built in Shoreditch about the year 1570: the one was called 'The Theatre,' by way of distinction, the other, 'The Curtain.' To-day there are at least fifty buildings licensed in London for dramatic representations. Of the history of the English stage between 1464 and this it is not my purpose now to speak.

I will only say in passing that that history brings before us dramatic writings which contain the noblest and purest literature, the best poetry, the finest sentiment, the most elevated morality, and the names of some of the purest men and women that have adorned English society. I would not forget to mention that the name of William Shakespeare belongs to that period, and that next to the English Bible his works stand as the crown and glory of our English literature.

I want now to say something of the influence of the theatre on the peoples and nations that have most patronized it, as also of its influence upon its actors.

There is no doubt that in Greece, under Thespis and Æschylus, Sophocles and Euripides, it was a great moral power, and that it had a most elevating effect upon the characters of its votaries. At that time both author and actor were men moving in the first ranks of society, many of them the makers of the best features of Grecian history. Æschylus and Sophocles were soldiers and statesmen, and yet were not above appearing on the public stage. But, alas! Greece gave her beautiful locks to the Delilah of impurity. From the beauty of Æschylus and the grandeur of Sophocles she went over to the fooleries of Aristophanes and the indecencies of a school of licentiousness, until not long before her fall the stage that could provide the greatest excesses, and depict scenes of the grossest immoralities, was the most flourishing and the most honoured. Her young men were corrupted, and her old men became senile *roués ;* the days of strength and heroism suggested by Homer and Æschylus, Salamis and Marathon, passed away like a dream, and the land that had produced such an army of orators, statesmen, poets, philosophers, despising the restraints of her noblest teachers, went into the shadow of death.

What the theatre was to Roman life and Roman morals may be gathered from an edict of one of the prætors, which stigmatized as infamous all who appeared on the stage either to speak or to act. St. Augustine tells us that 'the ancient Romans, accounting the art of stage-playing and the whole scene infamous, ordained that this sort of men should not only want the honour of other citizens, but also be disfranchised and thrust out of their tribe . . . because they would not suffer their vulgar sort of people to be defamed, disgraced or defiled with stage-players.' Tertullian says that the temples were united to theatres in order that superstition might patronize debauchery; and that they were dedicated to Bacchus and to Venus, the confederate deities of lust and intemperance.

Whatever may have been the cause, history at least makes this clear, that the Roman empire was swept away by a tide of impurity, and that her throne crumbled from the dry-rot of uncleanness, which had its mirror, if not its source, on the stage.

What the theatre has been to French life most of us know too well. France has given up her Bible—to a great extent given up her Christianity; her theatre takes the place of her Sabbath worship; the stage has overthrown the pulpit; the actor has supplanted the priest. We know with what filthy rubbish her dramatists seek to gorge their flippant *clientèle* —stupidity that English common-sense would mock at; impurity that English modesty would spurn from the stage.

Of the effects of the stage on our English life it is difficult to speak. I know that, as I have previously stated, it has been the source of some of our best literature; that connected with it have been some of our noblest characters; that from its proceeds many charitable and religious institutions have received invaluable help; that music and art, eloquence and poetry, have been mightily strengthened, developed, and ennobled by it. But I cannot close my eyes to the fact that it has also mightily fostered, encouraged, and produced profligacy, vice and impurity; that in the past it has not been friendly to religious life, religious thought, religious reverence—things of the highest importance to man, to society, to the world.

One sad fact connected with the history of the stage is, that, whatever may have been the merits or demerits of the drama, the actors for the most part have been men and women of most undesirable character.

Writing in 1775, Josiah Quincey says: 'The stage is the nursery of vice, and disseminates the seeds far and wide.' Rousseau, whose leanings were certainly not towards prudishness, remarks: 'I observe in general that the situation of an actor is a state of licentiousness and bad morals; that the men are abandoned to low practices; that the women lead a scandalous life.'

Mrs. Siddons, writing of her sister's marriage, says: 'I have lost one of the sweetest companions in the world . . . but I thank God she is off the stage.' What does this reveal, but that one of the purest women that has adorned the English stage was conscious of the fact that the surroundings of the stage were not congenial to the living of an ideal life?

Fanny Kemble, in an article in the *Atlantic Monthly*, describing her first appearance on the stage, which was made for the purpose of retrieving the decaying fortunes of her family, says: 'So my life was determined, and I devoted myself to a calling which I never liked or honoured, and about the very nature of which I have never been able to come to any decided opinion. It is in vain that the undoubted specific gifts of great actors and actresses are given for rightful exercise; in vain that Shakespeare's plays urge their imperative claim to the most perfect illustration they can receive from histrionic interpretation; a business which is incessant excitement and factitious emotion seems to me unworthy of a man; a business which is public exhibition unworthy of a woman. . . . But though I have never, I trust, been ungrateful for the powers of thus helping myself and others, or forgetful of the obligations I was under to do my appointed work conscientiously in every respect, or unmindful of the precious good regard of so many kind hearts it has won for me; though I have never lost one iota of my own intense delight in the act of rendering Shakespeare's creations, yet neither have I ever presented myself before an audience without a shrinking feeling of reluctance, or withdrawn from their presence without thinking the excitement I had undergone unhealthy and the personal exhibition odious.' Further, she says: 'The vapid vacuity of my Aunt Siddons' life had made a profound impression upon me: her apparent deadness and indifference to everything, which I attributed (unjustly perhaps) less to her advanced age than to what I supposed the withering and drying influence of the over-stimulating atmosphere of emotion, excitement, and admiration in which she had passed her life. Certain it is that such was my dread of the effect of my profession upon me that I added an earnest petition to my daily prayers that I might be defended from the evil influence I feared it might exercise upon me.'

That is a remarkable testimony of a remarkable woman, who was morally strong enough to resist the temptations of the stage, and I think it throws a flood of light upon the conditions and surroundings in which an actor's life is passed, and the temptations to which they are subject. How easy must the road to ruin be to a life lived in that atmosphere!

Joseph Hatton, in his 'Reminiscences of John L. Toole' (published 1888), speaking of comedians off the boards, says: 'Hypochondriacal and gloomy creatures occasionally, whose fun and animal spirits leave them with their stage dress; or dissolute profligates, whose irregularities are a proverb, and whose homes are a disgrace' (vol. i., p. 88).

One thanks God that he is able to present Mr. Toole as a noble exception. So far as I know, the vilest breath of slander has never been breathed on his stainless name. Doubtless, too, the same might be said of many illustrious souls who have adorned the stage, adorned society, and adorned humanity, not alone by their abilities, but by their nobility of character. But that this is not so generally any-one knows who has taken the trouble to look and think for himself. Why? Is it because persons who take to the stage are naturally worse than others? Have they more of the brute and less of the human in them than their fellow-mortals? No; in my opinion it may be accounted for by the influence which their profession sheds upon them, and by the surroundings, physical and moral, in which theatrical life is necessarily passed under existing conditions. That those conditions are necessary conditions; that they are inseparable from histrionic interpretation and histrionic art, I do not for one moment believe. It cannot be necessary that the 'green-room' should be the door to vice; it cannot be necessary that an atmosphere of immorality should pervade theatrical surroundings. I see no reason why public-houses and dram-shops should attach themselves to the theatre: I see no absolute reason why loose characters should hang around the theatre any more than around a lecture-hall or a concert-room. That these things prevail is the disgrace of our modern civilization—an ulcer on the fair face of our national life. That much is being done in the way of reform I cheerfully admit, and am profoundly grateful for; that much more will be done I have a sure and well-grounded hope.

It only remains now for me to deal with the question which I am being constantly asked: 'Ought a Christian man, a Christian woman, to go to the theatre?' I will base my answer upon the principle laid down by St. Paul. I will say first that if a man's conscience tells him it is wrong, then for that man it is wrong. 'To him that esteemeth anything to be unclean, to him it is unclean.' If it gives you impure thoughts, low ideals, unholy desires, your bounden duty is to shun the place as though it were a lazar-house. If, too, your going would be a source of pain to your noble-minded wife, your modest sister, your sainted mother, as a Christian man you are bound to abstain from going. If it will lower your influence with your children, your employers, or those in any way committed to your trust, I would say your duty is abstention. But if, on the other hand, it is a pure source of pleasure to you; if it gives you lofty ideals; if it educates your taste for art; if it improves your musical culture; if it softens the hard places in life; if it soothes the jaded brain; if it interprets to you any of the mysteries of life, or makes you look thoughtfully at the solemnities of death, and no one is thereby offended or made weak, then, who but your Master dares judge you in that which you do? I, at least, will not be your judge. Tens of thousands of pure-minded, sweet-souled, Christ-loving men and women go, and know that they are none the worse for so doing. Who dares condemn them?

But there is a duty that, to the Christian, extends beyond self, self-interest, and personal relationships : the duty of the Christian extends to the wide circle of society, and to the yet wider circle of the whole community. That duty should compel every Christian to demand pure plays. I know that the State exercises a kind of censorship over the stage, as over the press; but much of that which passes the coarse-meshed sieve of State regulation ought not to pass the finer sentiment of Christian feeling. Against much of the 'up-to-date' nonsense that is put on the boards; against the immoralities that are veiled under a thin gauze of doubtful modesty; against the dramas that demand for their interpretation unwomanly exhibitions, unmanly fooleries, it is the duty of the Christian Church and the Christian world to lift up its voice and to protest. And I say to strong-minded, pure-souled men and women that, instead of allowing bad plays to be acted before bad people, making actor and spectator ten times worse than they otherwise would be, it were better that you should go to these theatres, hiss down the actors, cry 'Shame!' at their immodesties, and agitate against them until they reform or perish. The Church is strong enough to blot out the worst plays that were ever written.

Further, this Christian principle should compel us to discountenance in others that which we would not tolerate in ourselves.

In the name of all that is true and beautiful I object to much of the garb of the stage. I am no prude; I am no Philistine; but for decency's sake I am bound to protest against the shameless displays and the immodest representations of semi-nudity so often to be seen. No man would tolerate it in his home, and we ought not to tolerate it in the theatre. How many of you parents would like to see your daughters go on the stage in a fashionable ballet? To manage the feet in such an unobtrusive manner, to revolve so gracefully, and poise so artistically, is doubtless clever, and those who do it may be refined and pure souls, but would you like your child or your wife to do it? If not, you have no right to countenance it. You need not judge others, but you yourself are bound to stay away. That which is ignoble for the actor is ignoble for the spectator. That which is wrong on the stage is wrong in the stalls.

If Christian men and women would act on these principles we might soon have a pure drama, a modest stage, noble actors and actresses, and pure surroundings; and, instead of the complaint that the theatre is the nursery of vice, the source of evil, and the well-spring of licentiousness, we should soon hear of it as the minister to a legitimate want, the centre of a pure and pleasurable influence, the creator of lofty ideals, the friend of philanthropy, and the handmaid of religion.

> 'The drama's laws the drama's patrons give;
> For those who live to please must please to live.'

The Church, therefore, holds the key of the situation. God help us to do our duty!

Politics

IN THE LIGHT OF CHRISTIAN ETHICS.

St. John xviii. 36.

'My kingdom is not of this world.'

Revelation xi. 15.

'The kingdoms of this world are become the kingdoms of our Lord, and of His Christ; and He shall reign for ever and ever.'

POLITICS

IN THE LIGHT OF CHRISTIAN ETHICS.

INCALCULABLE mischief has been done by the supposition that the first of these texts is an emphatic declaration on the part of our Lord that His religion was to have nothing to do with earthly, worldly, and material things. And the men who have held this mischievous doctrine have bolstered up their mischief by an appeal to the fact that Christ Himself took no part in the public life of His time, and that His disciples and apostles held themselves sternly aloof from all the political movements and activities of their time. In regard to my text, let me say that, when our Lord asserted that His kingdom was not of this world, He did not mean that His religion was not to touch the many-sidedness of the world's life. He was in the presence of Pilate, who was trying to draw from Him some statement of His authority to act as He had been acting, some defence of His extraordinary conduct, some excuse for His revolutionary teaching. 'What hast Thou done?' asks the representative of Rome's imperial power. My kingdom—that is, My authority to do as I have done—is not of this world. That is a very different thing from saying that His kingdom was not meant to rule over this world.

In regard to the fact that neither He nor His Apostles took any part in the public life of their time, I would say that it was impossible for them to do so, not because it would have been alien to their purpose, but because there was no opportunity for such a line of action. 'The whole of Europe and Asia, under the Roman Empire, was governed despotically, and there was no room for individual citizen activity.'

Those who were accounted rulers in Palestine—the Herods and their sanhedrim—were only puppets, tools of that mighty engine of power Imperial Rome.

There is, on the other hand, every evidence that the Christ intended His kingdom to embrace all interests, and to transfuse and transform every dominant power of the world.

He began His ministry in the synagogue at Nazareth by connecting Himself with that prophetic statement of Isaiah's which told of that coming King who should be the means of setting right the wrongs of earth, and turning the wayward feet of men into paths which should lead them to higher destinies and nobler conditions of life. 'He hath sent Me to heal the broken-hearted, to preach deliverance to the captives, and recovering of sight to the blind, to set at liberty them that are bruised, to preach the acceptable year of the Lord.' That is one of the most striking political statements ever made. It was a political programme mapped out by the great evangelical prophet; and He who came to fulfil the prophets took it up as His own work: the whole of His life and teaching was the carrying out of this programme. And, 'though He had nothing to do with the despotic government of His day; though He left the Herods and the Cæsars alone, to perish as they deserved to perish, He yet infused into every soul that believed in Him a power which was meant to literally take possession of all the reins of government upon earth, and administer this world in the Name of the King to Whom it belonged.'

'Think not,' He said, 'that I am come to send peace on the earth'—to acquiesce in things as they are, to treat the world as though it were beyond My notice—' I came not to send peace, but a sword;' came to be a revolutionist, a reformer, a political creator, a breaker down, and a builder up.

There is every evidence that His apostles who succeeded Him took the same view of His mission, and the ultimate object of His kingdom. Their writings are not only impregnated with maxims and principles that apply to the community, and through the community to the commonwealth and the body politic, but they contemplate the triumph of the Christ over every power, temporal and spiritual alike. They not only speak of their Lord as King, but they ascribe Kingly functions, Kingly powers, and Kingly rule to Him. St. Paul says, 'He must reign till He hath put all enemies under His feet.' And in that apocalyptic vision in which the sainted Seer saw the final consummation of all rule, and all authority and power, he says, 'There were voices in heaven saying: The kingdoms of this world are become the kingdoms of our Lord and of His Christ; and He shall reign for ever and ever.'

The Roman Church rushed into the extreme of supposing that this was meant to be a literal prophecy of a personal temporal reign on earth, and that, as the person of the Sovereign King is in heaven, His vicegerent must take His place on earth. And hence for centuries the Bishop of Rome was regarded and revered as Christ's representative on the thrones of the world—' King of kings and Lord of lords.' The Roman Church is still hoping and still labouring that that power may be regained. That is, I think, prostituting a magnificent truth into an egregious falsehood: replacing a Divine reality by a human fictitious absurdity.

Christ's rule over temporal things is precisely what it is over spiritual things, not the suppression of individuality, but the suffusion of all faculties, functions, and powers with His Spirit, His life, His elements of character, His grace, and His beauty. He is to rule in the earth, not by deposing the powers that be, and placing on their thrones men with delegated powers from Him; but by filling the powers that be with His Spirit, and moulding them after His image. By possessing human hearts He will become humanity's King.

He may thus be the great political Leader of the world; over monarchical and republican governments alike He may preside; through all forms of political economies He may lead the generations on to nobler destinies and more perfect conditions of life. That, I take it, is His mission in the world to-day: that is the mission of Christianity, so far as it applies to mundane and temporal things. You will, therefore, readily see that the Christian man, far from being out of place in the political world, is really promoting his Master's kingdom, if he carries into that world the spirit of his Master, and seeks to apply His Divine ethics to the exigencies of political life. It is through the Christ-spirit in the individual, manifested in every phase of life, that the universal triumph of Christianity is to be assured. All the economics, therefore, of the body politic ought to be in the hands of Christian men, determined to deal with them in the spirit of Christ, and in the light of His Divine revelation.

It is one of the curses of our modern life that politics, like most other mundane matters, have been divorced from Christian living and Christian life. So much is this the case that men have got to look upon an ardent politician as a man almost opposed to religion, almost necessarily without religion: to dabble in politics is to forswear Christianity. Such a conception is as stupid as it is erroneous. The world of politics may be as sacred as the world of art, of science, or even of religion. Governmental affairs are as Divine as Theological affairs, and the righteous politician may be as much a servant of God as the deacon or the priest; the Premier of a nation's Parliament may be the promoter of Christ's kingdom as much as the Primate of a nation's Church.

Men make a vital mistake when they concern themselves with matters religious, and neglect matters political; they wholly mistake the purpose of God when they pronounce the Church sacred and the forum profane; they have not learnt the spirit of Christ when they think that religion and politics have nothing in common. Everything that affects humanity's well-being, that is elevating, that tends to improve human conditions, to prevent suffering, to secure the greatest good to the greatest number, is certainly religious, is truly Christian. Government under existing conditions is an absolute necessity; he, therefore, most serves his

Master who helps to make government righteous, and seeks to apply the maxims of Christianity to the economics of legislation.

The ban of our modern political life is that men enter it, and support it, from every motive but the right one. The forum is full of place-seekers, tuft-hunters; men who care nothing for principles, but everything for power; nothing for measures, but everything for party. The wretched divisions of political life make righteous legislation almost an impossibility. What James Russell Lowell wrote of Party Politics in America in 1846, in those wonderful and inimitable papers called the 'Biglow Papers,' he might write of many English politicians to-day:

> 'Gineral C. is a dreffle smart man :
>   He's ben on all sides thet gives places or pelf;
> But consistency still wuz a part of his plan,—
>   He's ben true to *one* party—an' thet is himself;
>   So John P.
>   Robinson he
>   Sez he shall vote for Gineral C.
>
> 'Gineral C. he goes in fer the war;
>   He don't vally principle more'n an old cud;
> What did God make us raytional creeters fer,
>   But glory an' gunpowder, plunder an' blood?
>   So John P.
>   Robinson he
>   Sez he shall vote for Gineral C.
>
> 'We were gittin' on nicely up here to our village,
>   With good old idees o' wut's right and wut aint,
> We kind o' thought Christ went agin war an' pillage,
>   An' that eppyletts worn't the best mark of a saint;
>   But John P.
>   Robinson he
>   Sez this kind o' thing's an exploded idee.'

Yes; everything's 'an exploded idee' that doesn't suit party politics. A good proportion of our politicians might, to quote Lowell again, thank Heaven that

> 'A marciful Providunce fashioned us holler
> O' purpose thet we might our principles swaller.'

That ought not so to be. A politician ought to be as reliable, as straightforward, as honourable, as charitable, as pure-minded, as a priest. And where he is not so, the man is by that very fact disqualified for his high calling. I do not say that the Christian spirit will make all men think alike, or see alike, or devise alike the same measures for the government of the commonwealth; but it will secure that charity that thinketh no evil, that rejoiceth not in iniquity, but rejoiceth in the truth—the charity that suffereth long and is kind.

A little more of it in the world would have prevented the pitiable sight of a stupid mob of fashionable gentility, at a royal reception, hissing a fellow-guest, an octogenarian statesman, who, whatever his faults, has done noble work for the English nation. Such abominable snobbism is a direct negation of the Christ-spirit and of Christianity. And yet that is but a fair sample of the intolerance, the conceit, the stupidity of party politics in the present day, and of all parties alike. I call upon the Church to do its utmost to eradicate this un-Christian element in our political life.

Competition will never be put down; it is one of the means whereby men arrive at the highest methods of progress, of usefulness, and of beneficence. But competition supported by lying, by meaningless promises, by vilification, and by ribaldry, must be put down. And if those avowing Christianity would set their faces against it, as it is their bounden duty to do, it *would* be put down in a decade.

I call upon all citizens to give to the politics of their time their most serious consideration; it is your duty, as citizens of that great empire in which God has placed you, to take your part in that wonderful economy which has made England one of the greatest nations of the earth. If you neglect this duty you will be as culpable as if you neglected your prayers, your worship in the House of God, your participation in those duties which you have always regarded as sacred. It is not enough to say, 'But politics are not in my line': that may be only an excuse for your selfishness. The father of a family might just as well say, 'The duties of a father are not in my line.' The fact of his fatherhood enforces those duties; the fact of your citizenship enforces yours. You cannot escape them, and if you neglect them, you sin. It is no use saying, 'Politics are rotten.' Politics are not rotten; the men who dabble in them may be, and it is your duty as a Christian man to see that the tuft-hunter, the place-seeker, the office-monger are supplanted by men of principle, men of honesty, men of true patriotism, men of sterling integrity. You may not agree with them, but their influence will tend to the ennobling of the nation, to the march of human progress, and to the dawn of the day when there shall be voices in heaven, and perchance on earth, saying, 'The kingdoms of this world are become the kingdoms of our Lord, and of His Christ.'

But I am to speak of the ethics of Christianity as applicable to the problems of modern politics. And in doing this I must state at the very onset that these ethics have a general rather than a particular application. You will find no specific rules for legislation, any more than for business, in the New Testament; but there are principles inculcated which were intended for the guidance and direction of both, as, indeed, for every phase of our common life. Take, for example, the great problem that is exercising men's minds as to whether it is right, equitable, fair, to disestablish and disendow the Anglican Church in this country and the Presbyterian Church in Scotland. The New Testament offers no manner of counsel on the question, but it does lay down general principles which we are bound to observe. Our Lord Himself, when appealed to in regard to a tribute paid to an alien king, and an alien government, laid down this universal principle: 'Render unto Cæsar the things that be Cæsar's, and unto God the things that be God's.' The matter of the tribute-money was nothing compared with the principle of justice and righteousness. That will have to be the foundation principle which must determine the rightness or wrongness of the question at issue. Whether it is expedient or not must be determined by the voice of the nation; whether it is right or not must be determined by the ethical maxims of the religion of Christ.

The great question of Home Rule for Ireland is a matter to which you can only apply the most general religious principles. There is not a single maxim to which you can point which makes it either right or wrong to grant Home Rule. Its rightness must be determined by its manifest expediency or inexpediency, and by its apparent effect upon the community. You have to weigh probabilities; to take into account the tendencies of human nature, the contingencies that may promote internecine strife; to consider well the fitness of a people for autonomy, and the possibilities of their ruling in righteousness. And having settled this, you have no appeal to Scripture, or to any law, human or Divine. The question must be wholly determined by the balance of human opinion; only it is your duty to see that that opinion be impregnated with the Christ-spirit, and expressed in brotherly charity.

All international questions must be settled upon the broad principles of justice, and upon the Christian principle, 'Thou shalt love thy neighbour as thyself.' From that there is no appeal. You dare not do to another nation that which you would not another nation should do to you.

When we come to the great problems connected with capital and labour, we have unmistakable Christian teaching for our guidance. It is the bounden duty of the legislature to see that justice is done to the toiler as well as to the employer; it is the bounden duty of the Christian community to see that our legislators recognise this solemn responsibility. The awful revelations made a short time ago in regard to the abominable sweating system ought to have been impossible in a Christian country. That the Church has not risen as with one voice to demand, through the legislature, the redress of these awful wrongs, will, in my opinion, ever remain as a bloodstain upon the robes in which she ministers to the people.

The Christianity of the New Testament is the champion of the weak against the strong, the poor against the rich, the oppressed against the oppressor. 'Behold, the hire of

the labourers who have reaped down your fields, which is
of you kept back by fraud, crieth : and the cries of them
which have reaped are entered into the ears of the Lord of
Sabaoth.' That cry to-day is going up from the sweater's
den, and it must be silenced by the championing voice of
Christianity, expressed through the constituencies of this
wealthy nation. Come what may, the hireling must not be
oppressed, the labourer must not be turned into a machine
for the burnishing of gold to gild the couch of slumber for
the rich.

One other matter which a Christian legislature ought to
make a primary question is the health and common decency
of the community. Nine-tenths of the working men and
women of this country are housed under conditions which
make modesty and decency impossible, and health pre-
carious. In London and our greater cities especially the
prevailing state of things is a disgrace to our civilization.
Men, women and children are herded together in rooms in
the vilest conditions—conditions such as any gentleman
would be ashamed to house his cattle under—and nobody
cares.

If any man in the world has a right to a decent, commodious, comfortable, healthy home, it is the working man
—the man who produces for us the necessaries as well as
the luxuries of life, and one of the duties of a Christian
community is to see that her toilers are cared for. The whole
of our land wants rousing on this great question, and it is
the duty of the Church to sound the trumpet-call; the duty
of every Christian man to lift up his voice in demand that
these wrongs may be redressed—to send to Parliament, to
our County Councils, and our public administrative bodies

generally, men pledged to work out these reforms. If we fail in that duty, if we appoint or reappoint men 'simply on the principle of idle party contests, or, still worse, on principles of pecuniary interest,' the Lord of Sabaoth, the God who careth for the poor, will visit His judgments upon us, and scathe us with rods of our own making.

I come now to the question which is occupying our thoughts to-day—the question of hospitals.

Here, of course, I leave the domain of practical politics. Alas! our charity has been as unworthy of us, as a nation, as have been our politics. We have avowedly made Christianity the basis of our national life; in name, at least, we are a Christian people. With that basis and that name we have grown to be the greatest nation in the world, with larger territory and greater influence, probably, than any people that ever lived. But while we have been thus growing, expanding, amassing, under the guise of Christianity, we have failed to keep the commandments of Christ; we have neglected the causes, the institutions that are most essentially allied with Christian life and with Christian endeavour.

What a comment upon our faith that we can carry on the ocean trade of all nations; can equip and send out an army on the shortest notice, and defend the honour of our country in the remotest corner of the globe; can supply the whole world with manufactured goods, and money, too, if they want it, but that we cannot find room for the suffering poor of our country; that we cannot prevent men dying of want, and in conditions of the most loathsome suffering, under the very shadow of our churches!

Of what use is it to boast that the wealth of the nation

is at the present moment about *two hundred and fifty pounds* per head; that during the past fifty years we have increased the value of our railway property by nearly one thousand million pounds, and our shipping by more than one thousand million pounds, when we cannot maintain the institutions which philanthropy has established for the alleviation of those ills, and the amelioration of those woes that oppress our brother-men?

What a tale it tells of our selfishness that every year, at the Derby, a million of money changes hands, and that in all the churches and chapels of London we can only collect the beggarly sum of forty thousand pounds for our hospitals! What a pitiable thought that this nation can spend one hundred and thirty million pounds in drink, and that it yet has to close many of the wards in our hospitals because it cannot afford to keep them open!

I appeal to you to do your duty. I ask that you will send such an offering to the hospitals of London as shall give the lie to the statement that Christianity, as an operant influence on the world's selfishness, is played out. I ask in the name of Him who gave His life for you that you will do your utmost for those institutions which are not only houses of healing for the sick poor, but are, by every influence which they are shedding upon the world, tending more and more to bind together the sons of men and to bring in the universal reign of Christ.

Society's Wastes

IN THE LIGHT OF CHRISTIAN ETHICS.

GALATIANS v. 13.

'By love serve one another.'

ROMANS xiv. 7.

'For none of us liveth to himself, and no man dieth to himself.'

SOCIETY'S WASTES

IN THE LIGHT OF CHRISTIAN ETHICS.

THESE two texts reveal to us St. Paul's conception of the solidarity of life. Not only had God made of one blood all the nations of men to dwell on all the face of the earth, as he told his hearers at Athens, but had in that one blood made them a concrete whole, with a unity of interest, unity of force for helpfulness, with the law of interdependence stamped upon the whole constitution of the race into societies, nations and kingdoms. 'None of us liveth to himself, and no man dieth unto himself.'

I want you to accept that as the underlying principle of life, and to have it in mind while I speak to you of the wastes of our modern social life. You cannot speak of human society except as embracing the concrete whole of human life. In the economy of life, as God ordained it, there are no classes and masses, no caste and distinction of high or low. I do not say that these things are opposed to the purposes of God, but only that they are not of His ordaining. He gave the race a solidarity so perfect that if one member suffer all the members suffer with it: we have elected to divide the race into classes, but that has not undone the solidarity. We cannot get away from the fact that every man is connected with every other man, and in that connection all bound to God.

Human society, in its broad sense, is 'that method under which men live together in all their interests, in their social relations, in their businesses, in their very conditions of poverty, or riches, or industry.' It ought, therefore, to be a common axiom that every member contribute something to every other member's good. That, if you will take the trouble to think, you will readily detect lies at the very basis of society, organized as it is, and as it is bound to be, on the principle of solidarity. A man's intrinsic value consists in the amount of his good-producing qualities; not only in what he is in himself as a moral being, but in what he is capable of doing for others—for the common weal.

It seems, too, that God has so regulated the varied and complex machinery of human society, so ordained the many economies of life, so distributed its forces, that, for the well-being of the whole, each must take his part in the things that contribute to the general good. And so plainly is this so that our estimate of a man ought to be determined, not by what he possesses, but by what he does; not by what he hoards, but by what he produces; not by his ancestry, but by his fulfilment of his high calling in the world's work. With this view of the economy of life—and I maintain it is the Bible view, the New Testament view, a rational view, and the only practical view—let us think

1. Of those wastes that arise out of false conceptions of life's duties.

I refer here especially to that ever-increasing class whose

only conception of living at all is living at the expense of others. You will find this conception at the two extremes of society—at its top and at its base. And if it is more reprehensible in one than in another, it is certainly in that at the top, because those at the top ought to have clearer vision, a more definite and accurate conception, of the duties of life than those at the bottom, many of whom are born mentally and morally blind, and never will rise above the conception of their own wants, and how to meet them with the least possible energy and trouble.

What are the facts? Why, that those who are born at the top, born with the fabled silver spoon in their mouth, born with every want of their animal nature supplied before the want existed, go through life for the most part as a caterpillar goes over a leaf—to get all it can out of it. They create nothing; they produce nothing; they add nothing to the sum of human comfort: they are simply the eaters, the appropriators, the users, the consumers of that which others create. It is not enough to say that they buy what they eat and drink and use; money is not the highest thing in life: it ought only to be a token of exchange between one form of good and another. No man can live on money, he can only hand it over as a token of value for the things which are the necessaries of life. And yet, sad as it is to recognise, there are thousands of men and women among what are called the upper classes who are thus so many parasites on the world's fruitful energies.

I thoroughly endorse the statement of one of the purest minds this century has produced—that 'every healthy man competent to work, but unwilling, who lives upon society without giving it an equivalent is a parasite.' I need hardly tell you what a parasite is : it is an animal organized to get its living out of somebody or something else—it does not work, it sucks for a living. The ant is a much nobler insect than the aphis. And every honest workman, doing honest work for honest wage, is a much nobler being than the idle aristocrat whose highest occupation is club-lounging, and whose noblest ambition is a carouse or a night of dissipation. The parasite of society calls the smock-frocked workman 'Hodge' and 'Chawbacon,' but, in the name of high Heaven, he is a nobler being than the yawning fop who sees no good in the world other than that which was made for his special delectation. Poor, white-handed, soft-boned, perfumed soul, he could not get in his own coals, or reap the corn for his own bread, if his life depended on it, and yet he dares call the man who does these things for him 'Chawbacon' and 'Hodge'!

I know that amongst the upper classes there are hundreds of brilliant exceptions to those I have been describing : men and women noble in act as well as in birth, and I would fain think that their numbers increase with the years ; but I know what I am talking about when I say that society, at the top, is full of these parasites, the worst feature being that, though parasites, they have the capacity for honest, useful, and noble endeavour.

Then, if we turn to the lower class, what do we find there? Why this : that every loafer in high life has a hundred imitators in low life. It is estimated that in Great Britain there are at least three millions belonging to what we *should* call the working-class, who yet are nothing more or less than human parasites, living on the food which other hands prepare for them. This mighty host, under the name of pauper, vagrant, criminal, idle and vicious, are scattered over the length and breadth of the land, living on the toil of those who produce, procure, or provide the necessaries of life. Like the London sewage, which, 'feculent and festering, swings heavily up and down the basin of the Thames with the ebb and flow of the tide,' these miserable beings flow through the springs and tides of our industries, making them foul with putrid uncleanness—both a waste and a burden in the economy of our national life.

I do not wonder that men are clamouring for some kind of reform; that, appalled at the awful inequalities that exist, they are saying that wrongs must be righted. In this who can fail to agree with them? But where I, for one, fail to agree is with the thousand and one theories that men are putting forth for the remedy of all these ills. They say that society is wrongly constituted; perhaps it is. They say that it may be made much better; probably. But when some great Panjandrum steps forth and says, 'I'm the man to do it,' I turn away with disgust. It is only the evolution of life and character, based upon the principle of the solidarity of interest that underlies all society, that will do it. Socialism will fail, politics will fail, education will fail, but the Christ principle—'Thou shalt love thy neighbour as thyself,' and 'Whatsoever ye would that men should do to you, do ye even so to them'—when woven into the warp and woof of all our economic life, that will succeed, and human society shall become fair and beautiful as the garden of the Lord.

2. The next waste of which I will speak is that arising out of the misappropriation and misapplication of energies.

One thing is certain, that no man can fill his proper place in creation, in society, until he finds out what that place is; he cannot do the best kind of work possible to him until he has ascertained for what his functions and faculties, his capacities and abilities are most fitted. Every man is gifted with a capacity for something, with ability to do something that shall specially contribute to the world's needs, and his first business is to find out just what those capacities and abilities are, and then to apply himself to their exercise. All his education and tuition should be along the line of developing, training, enlarging and perfecting those capacities, that when he finds his sphere he may go to it accomplished. Every man, too, should seek to devote his energies to that kind of work which will be, not only as meal to the barrel, and oil to the cruse, but a source of unceasing satisfaction all along the pilgrimage of life, till he reaches the city which hath foundations.

If you accept these as common-sense statements, think how terribly perverted and mistaken are the systems of education that prevail, and the motives that are directing men's application to their callings.

When children get away from 'the three R's,' how terribly mischievous is the course into which they are goaded by foolish parents and guardians! A girl, for instance, is compelled to learn music, and to apply herself to it with earnestness, while she has no more natural capacity for music, and no more desire for music, than for learning Chinese. Because foolish society expects it, she is doomed to endure it, and when her education is completed she has just music enough in her to madden those who have to listen to it. And yet the father glories in the fact that she 'studied under the best masters,' and that her music cost him so many pounds sterling! Poor deluded soul! if he had found out the natural bent of the child's mind, he would perhaps, at half the expense, have had her taught housekeeping and cooking, and she would have been turned into society fit at least for one thing: the making of a comfortable home for some domestic man! But now with her smattering of music, and botany, and Latin, and French, and history, and drawing, with no real knowledge of any of them, she is just a helpless toy-baby, who can make neither herself nor anyone else happy. The world is flooded with such poor useless creatures, who might have made something out in life, if they had been trained for one thing, and that thing the pursuit or acquirement for which natural capacities fitted them.

I have known boys compelled to learn drawing at school who after years of teaching could never draw a bull's foot or a goose's feather; whereas if the money spent on the drawing had been spent on teaching them mathematics, or chemistry, they might have excelled. It is a waste of God-given energy to compel the faculties to exercise themselves in matters for which they are not naturally fitted. You fathers, find out your boys' bent, and educate them accordingly.

Then, too, think of the mistaken notions that determine men's choice of their callings and professions. A man has three sons. He himself has climbed up out of life's low places. As a maker of soap, or a vendor of cheese, he has been successful. He buys himself luxuries and takes his place in society. Having done this, he thinks it would be a lowering for his sons to go into his business, to start where he started, and climb as he climbed. No; they must go into one of the gentlemanly professions.

'That fellow,' he says, 'is a bold, daring chap; I shall put him into the army.'

'His brother is an argumentative fellow, never happy unless he is disputing and quarrelling about odds; he shall go in for the law.

'Teddie, poor Teddie, good, conscientious, delicate boy; always says his prayers, you know; hasn't the head of the other two; isn't in it when they are about. I shall make a parson of him.'

And so poor Teddie, because he is good and says his prayers, is thrust into that sphere where more strength, more courage, more nerve-power, more brain force, more genius is needed than in any other calling on earth. Because he looks sickly, misguided women say he looks heavenly, and strong-minded men say, as they discuss his sermons, 'Did you ever hear such twaddle?' The one place on earth that ought to be graced with the finest qualities, the noblest souls, has been for generations almost monopolized by the weak, delicate, ungifted sons of the rich. They are not wolves in sheep's clothing, they are not false prophets, they are not hirelings, as noisy-voiced shouters would have us believe; they are only round men in square holes, pushed into a false position by the stupidity of their parents. And the Church has to suffer, society has to suffer, and the kingdom of God on the earth is hindered.

What is true of misapplication in the Church is true in a greater or lesser degree in all the professions. Some men are pushed into spheres that are above their capacity, others into spheres that not a single faculty in their nature fits them for, whereas if they had been put, at starting, in the right avenues, and under the right inspirations, they would not only have been useful, but their lives would have been like the outpouring of music.

Think of the briefless barristers, the practiceless doctors, the cureless clergy, the idle lawyers with which society is swarming! It isn't that they are lazy, or incapable, or weak-minded: it is because they have been thrust into a false position. As blacksmiths, farmers, navvies, tailors, they would have been brilliant successes. As they are they are abject failures—flotsam and jetsam on the tide of human society.

What is true of the higher grades is becoming daily more true of the lower grades. Young men brought up in villages and small towns, the children of men who have earned their living by hard and honest toil, are migrating by thousands to the metropolis, and to other cities, with one ambition dominant: namely, to earn a living and to wear a black coat in the earning of it. Their supreme idea is not, What am I fitted for? where can I be useful? how can I consecrate my faculties to the service of my fellows, my country, and my God? No; but, Where can I work and keep my hands white, wear patent-leather boots, and a silk hat? And hence our common industries—industries that once were the backbone of our country—are being pushed into foreign lands, and our cities and towns are crowded with out-at-elbow, seedy, cadaverous-looking men, who call themselves clerks out of work. London teems with them. There has to be a great light thrown on this question of the misdirection of energy. In the meantime we have to bear it as a waste and a burden.

3. The third waste of which I will speak is that arising from preventible sickness and untimely death.

We are only just waking up to the fact that the purpose of God in the creation is wholeness and health, soundness and perfectness in all those functions that pertain to the preservation of life; and that where these things are not there is a direct violation of the laws and the purposes of God.

It was said very recently, by a man who knew what he was saying, that the proper duration of human life is anywhere from eighty to one hundred years; that men are so organized and constructed that they have a right to expect that. And yet the average duration of human life is only about thirty-three years. Not long since it was only thirty years. Consider what a waste that is, when you take into account the fact that the first fifteen years of life are useless, so far as conducing to the universal good is concerned. The average life therefore has eighteen years of usefulness, when God meant it to have seventy years. All the labour and burden of tuition, all the disciplinary forces that have to be exercised during the period of infancy, adolescence, and youth, are put forth for the sake of eighteen years, when they might result in four times that number. Thus, one-fourth of the human race is bound to produce, to create, to provide the necessaries of life for the other three-fourths.

Why is this so? If it be not in the purpose and providence of God, whence is it? It is due to the prejudice and ignorance and indolence of society in regard to those laws that conduce to health and longevity; due to vice, due to carelessness, due to wilful neglect of the laws of existence.

The hospitals and infirmaries of the world, the lunatic

asylums of the world, are full of men, women, and children who ought not to be there, and would not be there if the laws of God had been observed, either in themselves or in their progenitors. For if you want to see the practical working of the moral law, 'I will visit the sins of the fathers upon the children unto the third and fourth generation of them that hate Me,' you have only to go to the hospitals and asylums. There you may see it writ large. And all is a waste that the goodwill of God never contemplated. The factors of sickness and premature death are not of His making, but man's.

A man goes to live in a badly-built, badly-drained house. He doesn't know that it is badly constructed; he only knows that he thinks it cheap. By-and-by his wife is smitten down with typhoid, and, after days of agony, dies. The clergyman comes in to condole with the man. He talks to him very piously about the mysterious providence of God, and charges him to submit, and to say, 'Thy will be done.' Why, merciful heavens! the providence of God had nothing whatever to do with it, and it wasn't the will of God at all. It is worse than pious folly to say it is the hand of God: it is foul sewer-gas, against which every man ought to protect himself.

And so three fourths of the sickness and ailments and weaknesses of the world are wastes and burdens—wastes and burdens to the sufferers, wastes and burdens to society, and wastes and burdens that need not be. I quote the words of one of our great medical authorities, Sir Joseph Fayrer, who said in my hearing, not long since:

'If the people could be taught to believe in the efficacy of pure air, pure water, cleanly dwellings, temperate habits, proper food, and clothing, and could be induced to make efforts to secure them; and if they could be taught to regard infective diseases as the scourge of uncleanliness, and of their own disregard of the simple laws of health . . . the result would be, not only greater usefulness and happiness, but better health and the saving of money.' Then he goes on to say: 'Preventible diseases, the result of insanitary conditions, still kill many thousands yearly—at least one hundred and forty thousand; and, considering the large number of cases of illness for each death, it has been calculated that seventy-eight million five hundred thousand of days of labour are lost in this country annually, which represents a loss in money of seven million seven hundred and seventy-five thousand pounds per year.'

Sir Benjamin W. Richardson, who followed Sir Joseph Fayrer, said he thought the estimate a very moderate one.

I want to say that it is the duty of the State, the duty of society, and the duty of the Church in particular to make these things known. Nay, more—to protest against the conditions that are producing these things, and to remedy them. It is the duty of every governing body, from the Imperial Parliament to that latest of our creations, the Parish Council, to see that all our citizens, noble and simple alike, are protected against every preventible cause of sickness, weakness, and wasting decay. The suffering that flows from vice will only be alleviated and prevented by moral and spiritual forces. There the work of the Church begins; there is the sphere of the on-coming kingdom of God that will accrue on the reign of righteousness. And in the hastening of its coming you and I must each take our part by being righteous and pure and clean; by passing on pure influences, pure laws to our children, and to those who succeed us ; by sweetening the flowing streams of life ; by charity, devotion, and piety ; by serving one another in love, and by ever remembering that 'none of us liveth to himself, and no man dieth to himself.'

I think the light is breaking, and that a fairer morn is dawning. I think I see on the horizon signs that the day is coming in which man shall be emancipated from those conditions that enslave, and burden, and oppress him. In that day shall the glory of the race be revealed, and all flesh shall see it together.

War

IN THE LIGHT OF CHRISTIAN ETHICS.

St. Luke ii. 14.

'Glory to God in the highest; and on earth peace.'

St. Matthew x. 34.

'Think not that I am come to send peace on earth: I came not to send peace, but a sword.'

WAR

IN THE LIGHT OF CHRISTIAN ETHICS.

AT first sight it would seem as if the key-note of the angels' song was not in accord with the purpose of Jesus in regard to His kingdom; but it will only be at first sight, if you will trouble to read with the seeking mind and the understanding heart. The superficial student of the Gospel message sees only in the advent of Jesus the dawn of a kingdom opposed to conflict and aggression and war; the open-minded and open-hearted student sees that kingdom as directly making for all these things. Jesus did not come into the world to produce peace at any price, but to establish peace as the result of righteousness. It was not peace instead of conflict that He came to bring, but peace born out of conflict. And of Him it is said: 'In righteousness He doth judge, and make war.'

It is a stupid mistake to suppose that the song of the angels was a promise of universal, unconditional peace: it was only a promise of peace on earth as a result of certain conditions. It must not be read, as it is erroneously translated in the Authorized Version, 'Peace on earth, and goodwill toward men.' No, but 'peace on earth to men of good-will.' That is its proper rendering. That is the only peace possible to righteousness.

Read the first public utterance of Jesus in the synagogue at Nazareth, if you would learn what was His own conception of the object of His mission to earth. Reading from the Prophet Isaiah that God's Messiah was to proclaim release to the captives, and to set at liberty them that are bruised, He claimed the prophecy as referring to His own work in the world. 'To-day,' He said, 'hath this Scripture been fulfilled in your ears.' He knew only too well what was implied in that mission. He could but foresee that it meant conflict; that before His banner should float over the nations, before the captive prisoners should be released, and the bruised by false systems set at liberty, much tumult and war and bloodshed must accrue. But, at whatever price, the mission must be accomplished. 'Think not that I am come to send peace on earth; I came not to send peace, but a sword.' Not that the sword was His mission, but that the sword would have to be employed in the fulfilling of His mission; not that war was a thing desirable in itself, but that war might be a necessity before righteous peace could be established—righteousness at all costs, even of war.

It may be contended that against this the teaching of the Sermon on the Mount stands as an abiding protest; that with its heavenly maxims: 'Love your enemies, bless them that curse you, do good to them that hate you, and pray for them which despitefully use you and persecute you'—and its holy benedictions: 'Blessed are the peacemakers, for they shall be called the children of God'—it interprets to us more fully and perfectly the genius of the heavenly kingdom. My answer to that is, that the maxims and benedictions of the Sermon on the Mount were not intended to apply to national, international, and inter-racial economics; they were intended for the governing and inspiring of conduct between man and man, as members of the new brotherhood of the heavenly kingdom. It is legislation for a family of equal rights, equal aspirations, and a common interest, rather than for an aggregate of nations, with nothing in common save the fact that they are human.

Christianity, as it comes from the lips of Christ, is the champion of right against wrong, of liberty as opposed to slavery, of justice as opposed to tyranny, of beneficent legislation as opposed to despotic misrule, even at the hazard of life itself. There is a tremendous lot of nonsense talked by pious platitudinarians about the *sacredness of human life*. There is one thing that is more sacred than life, and that is *duty*. The cause of right, rightness, and righteousness first; human life second. So it was with the Master, who laid down His life for His brethren; so was it with the early Christians, who loved not their lives unto death. There have been worse things in the history of mankind since the birth of Christ than some of the wars which have stained the earth with blood; and they are the hatred and oppression and tyranny which have made the wars a necessity.

I know, too, that it seems like a strange comment on the influence of Christianity that the nation of all others which calls itself Christian, and which, perhaps, more than any other nation has the right to call itself Christian, should be contemplating the possibility of war in almost every quarter of the globe. The war-spirit is in the very air; the clouds that hang over us seem to march as in battalions.

Any moment may find us plunged into the fiercest conflict that the nation was ever engaged in.

Let us see how far the maxims and ethics of Christianity would warrant our engaging in any of these wars. And to do this we must ascertain on what condition war is in any case—viewed in the light of the teachings of Jesus—defensible. When is man justified in going to war with his fellows?

One thing in my mind is indubitably clear, and that is that it can never be right to make war from causes of jealousy.

People and races of equal civilization and resources stand in the same relation to each other, morally, as brothers in a family; and to make war when one is jealous of the other's power, when that power is exercised humanely and righteously, were like two brothers fighting to the death because one was more prosperous than the other. If one of the brothers in the family turned bully, or tyrant, or oppressor of his family, or of any connected with them, then the silencing of the bully and the correction of the oppressor becomes a duty, even at the cost of blood. But war from motives of jealousy is nothing short of fratricide, and the nation which provokes it and incurs it, and strews the earth with the corpses of its own children, is guilty of the blood of its brother.

I was literally amazed, a short time since, at the cool manner in which the President of the United States of America spoke of the possibility of war with this country, as though it were a game of football, or a billiard match. I am in no position to judge as to the rights or wrongs of the question at issue. Whether England had placed covetous hands upon Venezuelan boundaries or not, I am not prepared to say. This much I must say, if I would be true to my convictions—that nothing but the defence of our most sacred possessions will ever justify us in drawing a sword or pointing a gun at our brethren across the sea; but if they insist on fighting, then, in my opinion, they forfeit every right to be called Christian, and deliberately violate the foundation elements of that holy religion which we profess to hold in common. All territorial adjustment of boundary lines ought to be made a matter of arbitration; and the sooner the great powers of the world determine that only in that way shall they be settled, the better it will be for the whole of mankind.

Again, I think the spirit and genius of Christianity are opposed to war waged for the sake of dominion.

Of all the wars which have scourged the earth, the wickedest have probably been those carried on solely in the interests of despotism. Imperial ambition has cursed the earth with cruelties, and dyed it deep with uncleansable blood. Precipitate and needless conflicts incited by the proud instincts of despotic rulers have robbed the world of some of its noblest sons, and filled the air with wailing from the widow and the orphan who would not be comforted. Passing by the wars of pre-Christian times, many of the wars of the Middle Ages were perpetrated in the spirit of the vilest barbarity, and, though, alas! often baptized with a Christian name, were in the interest of the most ignoble of the passions of mankind—the lust for power. Nothing can be clearer than that the boastfulness, the violence, the insolent self assertions, of the monarchs of the world who made war upon weaker races and nations were entirely alien to the spirit of Christ, and to the kingdom of Christ, even though they marched to battle with the Cross emblazoned on their banner.

The wars of the first Napoleon were designed, planned, and carried out solely with the greed of glory and the lust of empire which were characteristic of the whole life of that proud tyrant.

It is to be feared that our own hands are not wholly clean in this matter. We, as a nation, have been at times guilty of carnage and devastation in the interests of empire rather than in the interests of humanity. Our battalions have put their strong heels upon the weak necks of down-trodden races, that we might add another jewel to the imperial crown. And as often as we have done this we have stained our throne with blood, and taken the sparkle from the jewels that were already in the crown. Whatever our guilt in the past, we must be careful not to add to it in the present and in the future. The glory of power and the lust for dominance must never send an English soldier to shed the blood of an inferior race.

But all this granted—and I take it that it will be granted by the common-sense, and the reasonable religiousness of the nation as a whole—what are we to say of other pretexts for war, and other reasons for sending our armies into battle? Are we justified in maintaining our Army and Navy at the expense of the millions of money devoted to it every year? Are we warranted in inventing and making instruments of war that practically mean instruments of annihilation: in arming ourselves to the teeth, in building huge vessels that are simply floating mines of devastation, and then calling ourselves a Christian country?

My answer to that is an unqualified 'Yes,' provided we do not use these things in the causes which I have just now suggested, namely, jealousy and aggression. The first duty of a nation is to defend itself, its children, and its treasure. Either in the providence of God, or by the might of our own battalions, we have become heir to the richest parts of the surface of the earth. The empire of our Queen is the mightiest empire in the world. If we are doing our best to rule the races and peoples within that empire righteously, justly, humanely, and with a view to their progress, shall we not seek to guard our own? Shall we say to the first bellicose monarch who menaces us, 'I was mistaken in thinking I ruled by the providence of God; take thou the rule and do better'? Or if some aspirant to the throne of England invaded our shores, should we welcome him with hurrahs, or with the shot and shell of our mighty guns? My answer would be—and I think I should give it in the spirit of that religion which I profess—'Withdraw, or I fire.' The only sure guarantee of peace is perfect readiness for war.

I know that there are a great many who think otherwise; who say that we ought to rely upon the progress of civilization and the advance of Christianity to prevent war, and that it is wicked waste to devote so much money, and energy, and skill to preparation for war. 'Peace at any price' is the motto of these peace-ites. To be consistent they ought not to have a single bolt or lock on their doors: they ought to do nothing to prevent the access of the robber and the assassin to their homes: they ought to seek no protection in the law, or in the police, or in any of the many institutions which society has devised for its own defence. The army and navy are the bolts and bars, the doors and barriers, the police, and the law, for protecting our homeland, and its treasures otherwhere. And we should not hesitate to use them if our homes were in danger, or our treasures threatened. God expects us to defend ourselves. And we should be cowards and poltroons if we neglected so to do.

But there is another duty—equally sacred, equally binding—and that is the protection of the weak against the injustice of the strong. The spirit in man which does not allow him to see a woman ill-treated, or a child tortured, or a blind man turned out of his way, without interfering, that spirit when gathered into the aggregate of the national feeling says, 'Hands off the weak, the oppressed, the bound, or we fire!' And our firing in that case would be as righteous as our prayers; the booming of the guns would be as sacred an act as the uplifted psalm of worship.

Every war undertaken for the deliverance of captive men, for the manumitting of the serf, for the unshackling of the slave, has been a righteous war. That terrible struggle between the Northern and Southern States of America in the middle of this century, urged on by the North in the interest of the slave, and ending in the complete victory of the deliverers, was, in my opinion, an epoch-making war, putting an end to man's ownership of man, not only in the States of America, but wherever the religion of Jesus is professed, wherever civilization casts its shining light.

If there is one sentiment in our English songs of which I am more proud than another, it is that of the skipper in 'Jack's Yarn,' where he tells the white-faced planter who had come on board after his runaway Sambo that an English ship is the slave's refuge:

> 'Every man is free, he cries,
> Where the British colour flies.'

That result was certainly achieved by righteous war.

One of the great causes which, not long since, threatened Europe, and England especially, with war was the cry of an oppressed nation. The most revolting and fiendish excesses of cruelty that it is possible to conceive were being perpetrated day by day by the Turks upon the Armenians, and for no ostensible reason, so far as can be gathered, except that most damnable of all hatreds—the hatred of religion. For weeks these Mohammedan reptiles had been sweeping down upon quiet, peace-loving, Christian villages, ravishing their women, murdering their little children and their strong men, burning their homes, stealing their treasures, and leaving nothing behind them but ruin and death. In one village comprising two hundred souls, six only survived when the hateful band had done their devastating work. On every hand we read of infants being butchered like sheep, women so horribly treated that they welcomed the cruellest form of death as a consummation to be wished in preference to the vile outrages of the invaders.

If we had no interest in these Christians other than that of our common Christianity, and our common brotherhood, the wails of their murdered men and outraged women ought to impel us to interfere, even at the risk of war. But we have an interest in Armenia beyond that of mere brotherhood. When the Berlin Treaty was formulated, and the territorial rights and independence of certain small states in Southern Europe and Asia were defined, England distinctly told the Armenians that she would not leave them to the exclusive and dreaded domination of the Turk; she gave Armenia the right to look to her for protection. And not only so, but she has prevented Russia from giving the aid which she was, and is, quite prepared to give. I do not care to inquire what Armenia now thinks of us and our pledges; but with the cold-blooded, red-handed fanatic murdering the choicest of her sons by thousands, and ploughing them into the ground like carrion, her estimate of our Christianity and our honour cannot be very high! I do know what many honest-hearted, open-minded, Christian-principled people at home are saying that England is becoming a by-word and a reproach among the nations.

Oh, yes, believe me, there is something much worse than a righteous war, and that is cowardice, and silent acquiescence in tyranny and oppression. We have fought in many places and on many seas where we should not have fought, but in my opinion it is a greater sin to be passive, when, by virtue of our pledges, of our manhood, of our holy religion, we ought to be active. I quote, and fully endorse, the words of Mr. Ruskin on this question: 'I tell you that the principle of non-intervention . . . is as selfish and cruel as the worst frenzy of conquest, and differs from it only by being, not only malignant, but dastardly.'

In saying all this, I am not overlooking the horrors of war—with its groans of the living and its thirst of the dying, its crimson gore and its bleaching bones, its bereaved widows and orphaned children. But this notwithstanding, I would not only vote for the drawing of the sword, but would myself volunteer to hold aloft the banner of freedom, justice and brotherhood, should the opportunity occur.

Till the spirit of Christianity reigns among the nations; till tyranny, oppression, rapine and lust be banished; till man to man the world o'er acknowledge a common life with common interests, we must in the name of Christ maintain the rights of man and redress the wrongs of man, avoiding war where possible, but shrinking not from it where necessity demands it.

It is only by the uplifting and the Christianizing and the educating of the race that we shall bring in the day of sacred promise

> When swords no more, as it hath been,
> Are arbiters 'twixt men and men;
> But fellow-men, the wise and great,
> In council sweet shall arbitrate.
> The world will turn a brighter page,
> And enter on her golden age,
> When wasting wars for ever cease,
> And all her arts are arts of peace.
>
> .   .   .   .   .
>
> When nations meet in fond embrace,
> And in a compact sweet and strong
> Resolve to labour late and long
> Till every land shall bolt and bar
> Against the grim old tyrant WAR.

Gambling

IN THE LIGHT OF CHRISTIAN ETHICS.

St. Matthew xxii. 39.

'Jesus said. . . . Thou shalt love thy neighbour as thyself.'

GAMBLING

IN THE LIGHT OF CHRISTIAN ETHICS.

THIS commandment is declared by our Lord to be one of the two foundations on which all the pillars of religion and morality must rest. The sum total of all which is due from man to God as his Maker and Father, and from man to man as his brother, is expressed in the one word *Love*—God with all thy heart, and mind, and soul, and strength; man, as thyself. I venture to think that this second phase of the great commandment has oftentimes been misinterpreted and perverted. It has been quoted as though it meant, Despise self and respect your fellows; hate self and love your fellows; forget self and consider your fellows. It means nothing of the kind. It pre-supposes the highest self-respect, self-honour, self-reverence, self-consideration. It implies that all that man as a psychical, spiritual being is capable of is due first to himself; to plan his highest good, to control his highest energies, to direct his highest ideals, to plume the wings of his highest aspirations. And then it declares that the very same principle, the same controlling, directing, planning energy, is due from man to his neighbour, that is, his fellow-man, wherever found. It makes egoism the fountain-source of altruism, self-love the spring of philanthropy — 'Thou shalt love thy neighbour *as thyself.*'

As I discuss the question which I have chosen to bring before you, you will, I hope, see the bearing of this upon the arguments which I am about to adduce.

My subject is Horse-racing and Gambling, but it is with gambling that I want specially to deal. Against horse-racing in the abstract there is, I think, very little to be said without plunging into foolish and sentimental inanities. The only argument that it is possible to adduce against the practice is the argument of cruelty. There is no more reason why a man, or a body of men, should not prove which of two or of ten horses can run the fastest than there is why railway companies should not prove which engine is the speediest, or cyclists prove which is the champion wheelman, or our latest inventors prove which of two motor-cars is the faster. I am willing to own, too, that there is something very thrilling and exciting in the thought of a number of well-bred horses—lithe, sleek, gloriously-fashioned creatures — contending for the mastery. The horse, it seems to me, always comes next to man in gracefulness of motion, in dignity of form, and in intelligent participation in the exhilarating competitions of sport. What Shakespeare said of man :

> 'In form and moving how express and admirable!'

we may say almost equally of the horse. It is a mistake to speak of these noble creatures as belonging to the 'lower orders' of creation. I fully and completely endorse the statement once made by John Bright in the House of

Commons that 'there is no such thing as an inferior order of creation.'

If ever this noble animal is seen at his best, it is on the race-course, where the care and kindness and skill of man has brought it as near to perfection as animal-life is capable of attaining. It is quite conceivable, too, that the pleasure which man realizes in witnessing the contest the horses themselves realize in contesting. I dare say that whip and spur do inflict a great deal of pain. I fully believe that much more pain is frequently inflicted than is necessary for the testing of the horse's highest powers. But this notwithstanding, the cruelties of the race-course do not compare with the cruelties inflicted on bus-horses in the slippery streets of London, or on the skeletons—called horses—that are made to drag ploughs and waggons on many of the farms of the country. Some of the noblest horses on the turf do not need either whip or spur to excite them to the doing of their utmost.

We must recognise, too, that the practice of horse-racing is one which has taken a firm hold of our national life. The people of England are essentially sporting people. They have inherited the taste through a long line of ancestry: it has entered into their very blood, along with their love of country, love of kindred, love of home. 'This is a fine day, what shall we kill?' is the Frenchman's estimate of our sporting characteristic. There is, no doubt, a great deal of truth in it.

'"Tis true, 'tis pity, and pity 'tis 'tis true.'

But if the Englishman loves killing, it is not from motives of cruelty, which would brand him as of the devil—but from motives of adventure and the excitement of sport. And be the motives right or be they wrong, they have undoubtedly helped to form the English character, to mould the English taste, to develop English manhood, and to place the Englishman, as a physical being, in the forefront of humanity. A select committee of the House of Lords, appointed to consider the national custom of horse-racing, and to report the issue, made the following report:

'Your committee think it desirable that this amusement (horse-racing) should be upheld because it is in accordance with a long-established national taste; because it seems to bring together for a common object vast bodies of people in different parts of the country, and to promote intercourse between different classes of society; and because, without the stimulus which racing affords, it would be difficult, if not impossible, to maintain that purity of blood and standard of excellence which have rendered the breed of English horses superior to that of any other country in the world. The committee would, however, consider these advantages more than problematical *if they were to be unavoidably purchased by excessive gambling, and the vice and misery which it entails.*'

That is the opinion of a body of men who were considered by the Government of the country competent to form a just opinion on the matter. And with that opinion, as here expressed, the common-sense of the nation is mainly in accord. There is nothing in horse-racing opposed to our religious and moral principles: there is nothing opposed to our high sense of honour, refinement, and nobility. It is not to the horses or the turf that we must look for evil. If evil there be, it must lie in some other quarter.

It is to that other quarter that I now direct your attention. Turn back for a moment to the Report of the Lords' Committee. You will note that it concludes with this remarkable sentence: 'The committee would, however, consider those advantages more than problematical if they were to be unavoidably purchased by excessive gambling, and the vice and misery which it entails.' Are they so purchased? and is gambling, with its attendant vice and misery, an essential feature of horse-racing?

Let us not close our eyes to these two facts—that gambling is not the product of the race-course, and that it is not peculiar to the turf. That gambling is one of the most distinguished features of our race-meetings anyone who has ever visited a race-course must know. I cannot conceive a sight more humiliating, more opposed to the essentials of a high state of civilization, more inhuman and fiendish, than the betting-ring at a race. The jargon, the mad excitement, the whole atmosphere, is a blot upon our modern life. To the uninitiated the sights and sounds would be a hopeless riddle, and he might well imagine himself in the midst of pandemonium broken loose.

We remember how, when Alderman Tittums was advised at a race-meeting to put a 'pony' on the Admiral, he softly suggested that a more appropriate proceeding would be to put the Admiral on a pony. That illustrates the stupid jargon of the ring to the uninitiated.

But more is there than stupidity, more than mad buffoonery: there is vice of the most vicious character.

Mr. James Runciman, in an article in the *Contemporary*

Review, on the Ethics of the turf, says: 'To the racecourse flows, without restraint, a full tide of the worst of men and the most debased of women. It may be that there is not a spot above the depths of hell which exhibits such a concentration of all that is sensual and devilish as the racecourse.' That is very plain speaking, but it is undoubtedly warranted by facts. It is very evident that gambling is the prime object of the gathering of this huge vicious mass.

Charles Kingsley said: 'Even before I thought seriously at all I found myself forced to turn my back on racecourses; not because I did not love to see horses run, but because I found that they tempted me to betting, and that betting tempted me to company and passions unworthy, not merely of a scholar and gentleman, but of an honest and rational bargeman or collier.'

Lord Beaconsfield said: 'The turf is a vast engine of national demoralization'; and of course he meant by the turf the gambling that is associated with it. It is not horse-racing pure and simple that draws these huge masses, but the excitement of betting. On the Derby Day at Epsom alone every year something like a million of money changes hands over the hazards of the turf.

Mr. Labouchere, writing in *Truth*, says: 'Every racecourse in the country is a gambling establishment.' The *Speaker* says: 'It is the curse of no small proportion of the people of this country.' Dean Hole says: 'It defies religion, degrades manhood, and spoils sport.'

Let us see where the root of this great evil lies. I have said that gambling is not the product of, nor peculiar to, the turf. In the last century it was carried to so great a length that men betted literally on everything. Horace

Walpole tells a story of a man who was taken ill in a tavern, whereupon odds were instantly given on the chance of his recovery, and the spectators refused to send for a doctor because it might prejudice betting. But then the custom was mainly confined to one class—the upper. To-day it permeates the whole of society. Princes gamble and peasants gamble. The heir to the throne, in the royal enclosure at Epsom, lays his bet; Mary Ann, in the kitchen of the suburban villa, lays hers. The clerk does it, the chimney-sweep does it, the merchant does it, the loafer does it.

But wherein lies the harm? There be those who say that there is no more harm in laying points on a horse than in insuring your life, which is a species of betting—at any rate, it is giving or taking hazards. This is very shallow reasoning, and I will endeavour, in the light of Christian ethics, to show you wherein the harm lies.

Let us be clear as to what we mean by Gambling. Distrustful of my own powers of definition, I will give you the definition of one of the master-minds of the age. Herbert Spencer says: 'Gambling is a kind of action by which pleasure is obtained at the cost of pain to another. It affords no equivalent to the general good: the happiness of the winner implies the misery of the loser.' That is a definition which, I presume, no one will be inclined to dispute. It is clear, succinct, admirable. Let us look at it.

Gambling affords no equivalent to the general good, *i.e.* it makes money a non-productive agent. If the whole wealth of the world were gambled, the world would soon be reduced to starvation. 'Money is a mark of civilization'; I do not care what form the money takes, whether gold, silver, copper, paper, or any other token that may be chosen as a substitute for these. To have exchange, commerce and trade, you must have a recognised standard of money. One of the tenets of civilization is that so much money shall represent so much of that which is essential to life. A man builds a house, the materials and labour of which represent the value of so much money, and the taking of the money for the house is a perfectly just transaction. Another grows on his land so much corn, by which men live; the receiving of the standard value of the corn in money is an honourable thing. Another weaves or makes a garment; another writes a book that will be an intellectual help or pleasure to the community; society says garments and books are worth so much current coin, and the weaver, the tailor, the literary man, are regarded as honourable men when they give so much product for so much remuneration.

But what of the gambler? Does he contribute anything to the general good? When he has filled his purse with the results of a horse-race what has he left behind for the person whose money he has received? For whatever the gambler puts into his pocket is taken directly out of the pocket of somebody else, *and nothing is returned to take its place.* The winner has neither thought nor laboured; like the fowls of the air, he toils not nor spins, and yet he loads his pocket with that which society says must represent an equivalent in the economy of social life. So that from an economical point of view the gambler is a thief if he wins and a fool if he loses. In the former case he gives nothing for what he receives, which is tantamount to stealing; in the latter case he receives nothing for what he gives, which is tantamount to fooling.

But let us go further. 'The happiness of the winner

implies the misery of the loser,' says Spencer. You can't say that of any form of honest dealing. There may be, and ought to be, satisfaction on both sides when so much money is handed over for so much goods. Well, now place it beside this foundation of religion—'Thou shalt love thy neighbour as thyself.'

One thing we must recognise as an essential of gambling is that more than one must be a party to it : if you gamble at all, you must gamble with somebody. A man may indulge in the vice of drunkenness, and be the only party to the sin ; another may be a hateful liar, and affect nobody but himself by his lying ; but if a man is to be a gambler, he must either have a victim or be the victim. If he stakes more than he can afford to lose, and loses, he victimizes himself ; if he wins more than the other can afford to spare, he makes him the victim.

I am not now dealing with petty sums, though the economical phase of the question condemns even those. If a man is fond of horses, and fond of seeing the noble creatures contesting on the turf, and puts a small sum—say a portion of his day's pocket-money—on his favourite, if he loses he has derived so much pleasure from the transaction, which, by straining a point, we might say was an equivalent for the money spent ; but if he does—what is done tens of thousands of times every year—stake more than he can afford to stake, and lose more than he can afford to lose, then if he wins he robs his neighbour, and if he loses he robs himself —both cases being direct negations of the Divine principle, 'Thou shalt love thy neighbour as thyself.'

There is a bookmaker in this country whose annual turnover is a quarter of a million, and whose annual profits are sixty thousand pounds. Whence comes that? I say without fear of contradiction, From men who for the most part cannot afford to lose it. If I could only show you what that means, you could have no doubt whatever as to the unchristian character of this terrible habit. Youths who have rifled their employers' cash-boxes, thrown into the world characterless, penniless; wives and children brought to shame by the folly of the husband and father; homes filled with tears, misery and anguish; suicides who have wrung their hands in ineffectual lamentation in the face of the Baal-god of Luck — all the direct offspring of this wretched system. And this not in isolated cases, but in hundreds and thousands of cases.

If you want to know to what extent the evil has grown, and is growing, go into Fleet Street any afternoon when any great race is coming off, and see the mobs who eagerly watch the windows where the sporting papers are published, waiting for the declaration of the result. Note the haggard look on some of their faces, as I have done, a look that has ruin and suicide in it!

I know that the turf is not the only source and means of gambling. I have heard of such places as Monte-Carlo, Baden-Baden and Ostend, and I know something of what goes on there. In connection with the first-mentioned, there is a cemetery known as 'the suicides' cemetery,' where they bury out of sight the hapless victims of their pernicious systems. That fact is eloquent in itself.

Our own London Stock Exchange—'the great ganglion in which the nerves of the business world meet'—is permeated with the gambling spirit, as any honest stockbroker would tell you. All brokers are not gamblers; some of them are very honourable, just, upright Christian men; but that gambling goes on on the Stock Exchange, to the extent of millions every year, is perfectly well known in the commercial world.

I know, too, that much of the best and most manly sport in England is made the occasion of gambling. Men lay heavy odds on those who practise the art of self-defence, on teams in a football match, on two players at billiards, on the chances of cards—all as foolish as it is pernicious.

And because it is foolish, pernicious, unmanly, unheavenly, unchristian, undivine, opposed to the foundation principles of society, of economics, of morality and of religion, I am going to ask you to forswear it. Even trifles light as air sometimes lead to great issues. I am not going to condemn you for small points at a friendly game, or a pair of gloves on a race-course; but I am going to ask you to do your utmost to free our land, our commerce, our innocent amusements and our great national sport, from this awful blight which is settling down upon them, a blight full of plague-germs as pestilential as the Black Death.

If England is to have her pure manhood sullied, her commerce undermined, her trade shackled, and her sport and amusement contaminated by this plague-spot, then I say the price is too high. Better do without our race-meetings than maintain them to fill our cemeteries with suicides' graves, and to devastate the homes of England by ruinous losses on the turf. The conclusion of the Lords' Committee was a just one: 'The advantages are more than problematical if they are to be unavoidably purchased by excessive gambling, and the vice and misery which it entails.' We must appeal to the Christianized common-sense of men to strangle this hydra-headed monster.

As this is the first Sunday in the New Year, I give you these lines—from one of the sweetest, most manly singers of our day—as most eminently befitting both the occasion and the subject with which I have been dealing:

> 'One song for thee, New Year,
>   One universal prayer:
> Teach us—all other teaching far above—
> To hide dark Hate beneath the wings of Love;
> To slay all hatred, strife,
> And live the larger life!
> To bind the wounds that bleed;
>   To lift the fallen, lead the blind—
> As only love can lead—
>   To live for all mankind!
>
> 'Teach us, New Year, to be
> Free men among the free,
> Our only master Duty; with no God
> Save one—our Maker; monarchs of the sod!
> Teach us, with all its might,
> Its darkness and its light;
> Its heart-beats tremulous,
>   Its grief, its gloom,
> Its beauty and its bloom—
>   God made the world for us!'

London Problems

IN THE LIGHT OF CHRISTIAN ETHICS.

REVELATION xxi. 2, 3.

'And I, John, saw **the** holy city, **New** Jerusalem, coming down from God **out of** heaven, prepared as a bride adorned for **her** husband. And I heard a great voice **out** of heaven, saying, Behold, the tabernacle of God is with men, and He will dwell **with** them, and they shall be His people, **and God** Himself **shall** be with them, and be their God.'

LONDON PROBLEMS

IN THE LIGHT OF CHRISTIAN ETHICS.

I WANT first to correct a very sorry error that most people fall into when they read this chapter, and especially this description of what St. John calls the New Jerusalem, and that is to imagine that it has reference to a future world, a final heaven outside the confines of this little earth. Look again, 'I saw the holy city coming down from God *out of heaven.*' It was a place of habitation for the sons of men on earth after that God had long dealt with them. The nations going into it and coming out of it are those who are being saved. The inhabitants are those who are in a state of salvation. The city—large, vast, commodious—stretched over an area wide enough to be called a country, and lifted itself towards heaven as high as a mountain range. It bore, too, living and imperishable marks of the Old and New Testaments. People went in and out of it by gates which bore the names of the twelve tribes of Israel, while the foundations of the city were inscribed with the names of the twelve Apostles of the Lamb.

I know it is a vision, having nothing in heaven or in earth corresponding to it in literal reality, but it certainly is not a vision of the occupations and conditions of heaven and eternity as they are commonly understood; it is a vision of what man, and man's life, and man's cities, and man's world are to become through the work of Christ and the indwelling of God in humanity. It is not described as a city seen in heaven through some gate ajar, but a city which, from some lofty mountain, St. John saw come down out of heaven and locate itself here on earth.

Have we any realization of this glorious ideal among the many cities of the world? Is there one on this fair earth, seen from near, or seen from far, to which the wildest imagination could apply this glowing description of St. John's? No, no; but the tendency, thank God, is thitherward, and all progress—appallingly slow though it be—is towards that goal. Men are trying to sweeten the lives of great cities, trying at least to make room for the tabernacle of God, trying to make it possible to realize St. John's glorious ideal—'They shall hunger no more, neither thirst any more... and God shall wipe away all tears from their eyes.'

That conception underlies the very idea of setting apart one Sunday in the year as Citizen Sunday: and on that day, 'in the place where duty to God is enforced,' thinking of, and speaking of, our duty as citizens of this great city.

I want now to speak to you of the problems that confront us when we attempt anything towards the attaining of the ideal of the Apocalypse.

1. And first the vastness of London.

None but those who have tried to do something for the bettering of human conditions in London can have the smallest idea of how appalling is the vastness of this great city. Those who live in it and go up and down its streets have not the smallest idea of what is comprehended in that one word, London. Try for a moment and think what it means. Think of the four great capitals of Europe—Paris, Berlin, Vienna, and St. Petersburg—and it may help you to realize the vastness of London to know that there are nearly as many people within our metropolitan area as in all those four great cities put together. We are all proud of our colonial dependencies, but do you know that in the whole of that great tract Australia, New Zealand, Tasmania, and all the islands embraced under the term Australasia—a tract of country bigger than the whole of Europe—there are not so many souls as sleep every night within the area embraced by the word London? The same is true of Canada: the inhabitants of all its splendid cities, its flourishing towns, its thriving villages, its isolated homesteads, all put together do not equal the population of London.

Within the metropolitan area there are already seven thousand miles of streets, and yet each year fifty miles of new streets are added, and houses, not with pleasant breaks of greenery and surrounding gardens overlooking undulating meadows, but for the most part streets of houses joined one to another, and oftentimes with more than one family in a house. I have reminded you before of the cosmopolitan character of the inhabitants of London. Every nation and land, almost, upon which the sun shines has its representatives here, some in small numbers, some in huge multitudes. There are more Jews residing in London than in the whole of Palestine; there are more Roman Catholics here than in Rome itself, more Irishmen than in Belfast, more Scotchmen than in Aberdeen, more Welshmen than in Cardiff. And yet this huge cosmopolitan mass is adding on to itself, partly by immigration, and partly by the excess of the births over the deaths, seventy thousand new souls every year. Every four minutes of every day in the year a soul is born in London; every six minutes someone dies. In round numbers that means one hundred and twenty-three thousand births and eighty-seven thousand deaths every year.

Now, I ask, is any one mind capable of taking in all that is implied in the vastness of London? Think of the parishes, the districts, the centres of administration, the machinery for government, for the preservation of order, for securing anything like sanitary conditions, for supplying food, water, and other necessaries of life. Why, the very thought is overwhelming. To grapple with it is like having to grapple with a mountain range whose lofty peaks conceal one another, and whose rocky slopes contain chasms and crevasses that are only visible near at hand.

2. Think, again, of the terrible extremes and inequalities that exist in London.

This is by far and away the richest city in the world; its wealth in every form surpasses anything and everything that was ever got together in one place. Such vast and fabulous proportions has it reached that the mind is altogether inadequate to comprehend its bulk and the significance of its power. One of our ablest statesmen and statisticians told us some time ago that this country amassed its wealth more rapidly from A.D. 1800 to 1850 than in the whole of the eighteen hundred preceding years. That is to say, that we increased in riches more in the first fifty years of this century than from the time that Jesus the Christ lived to the year 1800. And yet—and it were almost past belief did not hard facts that nobody can gainsay stare us in the face —London increased its wealth more in the twenty years intervening between 1850 and 1870 than in the previous fifty years. It is calculated that we Londoners spend every year the vast sum of two hundred million pounds— this over and above what we save, and hoard, and invest. But this, for all practical purposes, is talking gibberish; the mind absolutely refuses to grasp the significance of such figures.

Let us look at the other side of the picture; that we may, perhaps, be able to take in and digest. Side by side with these gigantic strides in the march of commercial progress we have also, and keeping step along with it, the gaunt, ghastly, sickening skeleton form of the most degrading poverty. Rich as the metropolis is, rich beyond all possible means of computation, it yet has a poverty more hopeless, more bewildering, more maddening than anywhere else in the world. In the year 1896 the paupers of London—that is, those who applied for relief to the guardians of the poor —numbered one hundred and twenty-three thousand eight hundred and forty-four. That means that we have nearly three times as many paupers in London as they have in the whole of Wales. Added to this, it is computed that over half a million are supported or aided more or less by charity. Over and above these, again, there are thousands of little children—cursed, buffeted, neglected—who live by prowling in the markets, in the gutters, the railway arches, and the back slums of this awful city.

Think that the degraded women of London, who live for sin, and by sin—most wretched of all the wretched—equal the whole of the inhabitants of the city of Norwich! Think that the criminals of London equal the number of the inhabitants of Huntingdon! Think that its common lodging-houses herd together some twenty-seven thousand of the miserable social wrecks of life! Think that the number of those who live from day to day on the verge of destitution is probably as great as the inhabitants of that great northern city, Newcastle-upon-Tyne! Think that a third of the people of London are below the line of very poor! Think that one out of every five persons you meet in the streets will die in the workhouse, in the hospital, or in a lunatic asylum! Think that one million of our inhabitants live in one-roomed homes—men, women, and children all herding together like sheep in a pen! *Homes* did I call them? Is it fair to ascribe that sacred name to the place where filth predominates, and where decency is impossible?

Some time ago a contributor to one of our journals made a thorough examination of the conditions under which 'home work'—by which is meant wage-earning home work—is done in London. I will give you a brief synopsis of what he says, taken from one of our most sober-minded weeklies.

'Many of the houses of the home-workers were found to be in an extremely filthy state, and the work was carried on in them under highly insanitary conditions. Frequently one finds the home worker occupying an attic room at the top of a five-storied building, the ascent to which is by a dark and dilapidated staircase, infested, it may be, by rats, or haunted by that most pitiable of four-footed creatures, the slum cat.

At every landing narrow, grimy passages stretch to right and left, and on either side of these, close packed, is a row of "ticketed houses," that is, rooms on which the doors have marked on the outside the number of occupants allowed according to police regulations—regulations that are frequently evaded by means of that unknown and highly elastic quantity, the lodger. On every landing there is a water-tap and sink, both the common property of the tenants, and the latter usually emitting frightful effluvia. Probably the sink represents the entire sanitary system of the landing.

'Armed with a box of matches and a taper, and battling with what seem to be the almost solid smells of the place, one finally reaches the top, and on being admitted, finds, perhaps, a room almost destitute of furniture, the work lying in piles on the dirty floor, or doing duty as bedclothes for a bedridden invalid and the members of the family generally. In the case of one home worker, a shawl-fringer, where the extreme of poverty had apparently been reached, I found the sole furniture of the room was an old chair, a broken cradle, and some empty packing-cases.'

And all that here in London! Rich London! Fashionable London! Gay London! Giddy London!

You will, perhaps, suggest that this is a report of an exceptional district, and that the cases mentioned are exceptional cases. I tell you—and I speak of what I know—that neither the district nor the cases are exceptional. That report might be written of any twenty districts in London. I know it is true, because I have cases equally bad, and poverty equally appalling, in my own parish, and within three hundred yards of my own church!

I do not wonder that men say that all our show and glitter and glamour is very much like the shining structure of an old Mexican temple, reared upon a layer of living men flung in for a foundation. London certainly is not the city of God that St. John saw coming down out of heaven; we have rivers of tears unwiped, and hunger that is pinching, and biting, and consuming the flesh of thousands of our brothers and sisters, made, like ourselves, in the image of God!

3. Think now of the problem of rectifying, reforming, improving, annihilating these wrongs, vices, inequalities, injustices, and sins.

The Church is at work, philanthropy is at work, charity is at work—all saying, These things must not be, shall not be. But oh, what a hopeless, tangled mass it is! To unravel it looks almost as impossible as the dipping of the Thames dry with a teaspoon. Where to begin, what to do, how to do it, is the riddle and the puzzle. For, however well meant our intentions may be, unless we work on right lines we shall only make the tangle worse, and increase the evils that we want to remove.

The agencies of the Church, directly spiritual and moral, are at work, and with some measure of success, but yet only touching the very fringe of the gigantic fog of practical atheism. Philanthropy is devising all manner of schemes for the educating, and the enlightening, and the uplifting of the ignorant, the wayward, and the fallen; charity is sending white-winged angels of benefaction into homes of want, and yet, spite of it all, the evils continue.

One thing is certain: we have not yet solved the problem

of the best line of procedure. We are asking one another, Which is the better, to shut up the public-houses, and so take away from the drunkard some of the temptations to drunkenness, or leave these flaring, enticing places as they are, and teach the man manliness and self-control? And while we are wrangling over these questions thousands of drunkards die from the effects of drink every year. We have not made up our minds whether it is better to allow vice to parade the streets and secure its miserable victims in the eye of the public, or sweep it into privacy to hug its shame and its wickedness there. We do not know whether it is better to shut the poor up in workhouses and stamp them for ever with the mark of their poverty, or to minister to their wants in their own homes. These and endless other questions are vexing and perplexing and paining us, and meanwhile the roar and din of our folly and sin are entering into the ears of the Lord of Sabaoth.

Two things, I think, we are fully and firmly convinced of. One is, that we cannot make men wise, pure, just, and good by legislative enactments; that will only come by moral evolution, and by the indwelling of the Divine Spirit. We may get good and helpful laws on our side, but not all the laws ever formulated will make men wise, or build them up into a noble manhood. This will have to be done by spiritual and moral and intellectual agencies, and those agencies not professional alone, but general: the action of mind on mind, example on conduct, sympathy on emotions, and love on all. More holy characters is what we want, and more altruistic, selfless souls willing to live for men, and, if needs be, die for them; men willing to say with St. Francis Xavier:

> 'I want no heaven till all be Thine,
> No glory-crown, while work of mine
> Remaineth here; till earth shall shine
> > Amid the stars.
> Her sins wiped out, her captives free;
> For crown new work give Thou to me.'

Will you be one to say that?

The other thing we are firmly convinced about is, that indiscriminate charity, however well meant, is not only ill advised, but a positive factor of evil. To give money to the whining beggar in the street, or the plausible vagrant at your door, is to fee the devil to promote idleness, filth, and crime. No; whatever help is given should be given through recognised and accredited agencies, whose object it is to give help where help is needed and to stamp out professional vagabondism.

You will do well to make the Church your almoner. Help her to feed the hungry, to clothe the naked, to visit the afflicted, to comfort the sorrowful; and, if you care one jot for the approval of your Lord and Master, help with these words ringing in your ears: 'Inasmuch as ye did it unto one of the least of these, ye did it unto Me.'

Come, oh come, thou shining city of our God! thou holy Jerusalem! thou tearless, hungerless, thirstless, glory-encircled habitation for all the sons of men!

Labour Problems

IN THE LIGHT OF CHRISTIAN ETHICS.

ST. JAMES v. 4.

'Behold, the hire of the labourers, who have reaped down your fields, which is of you kept back by fraud, crieth: and the cries of them which have reaped are entered into the ears of the Lord of Sabaoth.'

LABOUR PROBLEMS

IN THE LIGHT OF CHRISTIAN ETHICS.

NOTHING that affects humanity in its social, commercial, and physical economics can ever be alien to the interests of Christian people. The Christian religion of to-day ought to be what the Jewish religion three thousand years ago was: the champion of the rights of man, the protestor against the wrongs of man, and the alleviator of the ills of man.

It is not enough to preach a Gospel that bears only upon man's destiny in the future life. The great want of the age is a Gospel bearing upon man's destiny and circumstances and condition in this life. It is not enough to provide what is called 'spiritual refreshment' for the souls of men. The wants of the body are as loud-crying, as assertive, and as imperative as the wants of the soul. And it is the business of the Church of Christ to see that the wants of both are met. He who preached peace to them that were afar off and to them that were near also said, 'I have compassion upon the multitude because they have been with Me now three days and have nothing to eat . . . . Give ye them to eat.' His religion is based upon the fact of the Divine

Fatherhood, which necessarily implies the human brotherhood of mankind. If there is one God and Father of us all, then there is a solidarity of interest as well as of life in the race, and one phase of the work of the Church is to point out what those interests are; to insist upon their recognition; to demand their just solution. That must be my excuse for bringing before you to-day the great problem of the relation of labour to capital.

This latter part of the nineteenth century has been called the 'age of the working-man.' If the importance of labour and the demands of the labourer upon those who share the fruits of his toil be what is meant, then it is the age of the working man. Clear is it that, whatever the age may be, the relation of capital and labour is the one problem that is struggling to find solution. The last ten years have clearly proved to us, not only that the problem demands solution, but that right-minded men of every class in society are resolutely determined that the problem shall be solved, and solved promptly and completely. For the first time probably in human history the gulf between the rich and the poor, between capital and labour, has been spanned with the golden bridge of far-reaching human sympathy. And to the credit of Christianity be it said, that not only has it laid the foundations of the bridge, but has been the very chains from which the bridge has been suspended between the two solid piers of humanity and charity.

During the conflict that has been waging between the labourer and the employer, between the hired and the hirer, certain facts have come to light which it is the interest and the duty of everyone to know, certain principles have been enunciated which you and I and every thinking man ought to ponder.

The system which has received most attention, and which has revealed the saddest features of the question, is that known as 'The Sweating System.' I may describe that system as the farming of human labour. Employers take contracts at an absurdly low rate, and then grind their employés down to long hours, low wages, and almost inhuman conditions of labour, in order to make profit out of their contracts.

Another fact which has been brought to light is the fact that an enormous amount of necessary and useful work is done at a rate of remuneration that does not serve to supply the absolute necessities of life; that after working twelve and fourteen hours a day for six days in the week, men and women are unable to earn sufficient to meet the barest wants of their nature.

A third fact has come into prominence: that the hours of labour in many of the most important industries are such as to make human pleasure and progress impossible, and existence itself almost unbearable.

Now, I am not here to discuss the merits or demerits of this or that particular phase of the commercial economics of the nation; I am not going to attempt to point out to you how these conditions have been brought about; but I am here as a teacher and a minister of the religion of Jesus the Christ to say that these things must not be, and that every Christian man and woman must use his and her influence to remedy these dire evils.

There are two principles which I am going to inculcate

as essentials to the well-being of the classes who live by the labour of their hands.

1. First, that all useful labour—and by that I mean labour devoted to things that supply the wants of mankind—should receive sufficient remuneration to enable the labourer to live.

In every case the principle ought to be recognised that the labourer is not only worthy of his hire, but worthy of such hire as shall supply him with all the requisites of life. Whatever is useful, whatever is beneficial, whatever is necessary, whatever is conducive to well-being, ought to pay the producer enough to provide him with the things necessary to existence. A working-man's only means of subsistence is his capacity for labour; where, therefore, he gives his labour, there he has a right to look for remuneration.

But the revelations of the last ten years have shown us that there are tens of thousands of cases where the whole time and energies of men and women are engaged, and where the wages paid are not sufficient to supply the commonest necessities of life.

A large number of men are employed in many departments of manufacture who work fourteen and sixteen hours a day, for the miserable sum of threepence per hour. A report issued a few years ago stated that the employés of the various omnibus and tramway companies throughout the country worked on an average sixteen hours a day, and that their average pay was never higher than threepence per hour; that thousands of the railway men in the kingdom were called upon at periods to work from thirteen to eighteen hours per day; that many of our metropolitan vestries employed street scavengers at only fourteen shillings per week ; and woman dust-sifters, who worked all day up to their waists in filth, for seven shillings per week.

A moment's thought must show you that, under such conditions, it is absolutely impossible that life should be anything but penurious drudgery. But there are worse conditions even than these in the employment of different forms of female labour.

In a reliable report relating to the employment of women in mills and factories, I read of a woman who at thirty-two years of age was a cotton-spinner, and had been at her work since she was nine years old. The report stated that she was making the magnificent sum of six and tenpence per week, and was supposed to live on sevenpence-worth of bread a week, taking peasemeal for dinner every day, except when she varied the diet with a halfpenny-worth of broth out of a coffee-house. When eggs were cheap she generally partook of an egg. An ounce of tea and one and a half pounds of sugar had to last her a week !

In Bermondsey there are hundreds of women employed as sack-makers, who receive sixpence per dozen for making sacks, and have to provide their own needles and thread. An expert says it is impossible to make more than from two to three dozen a day. A dock labourer's wife in Shadwell reports that for making twenty double-sewn nail sacks, which took her six hours, she only received the sum of sixpence. A report issued by the commission appointed to inquire into the 'Sweating System' reveals an awful state of things in regard to female work in the East End of London. In one case a woman works from six a.m to eight p.m., and does not clear one shilling per day. Another woman (a trouser-finisher) works from eight a.m. to eleven p.m., assisted by her daughter; the two together earn five and sixpence per week. Another woman (a shirt-machinist), working from eight a.m. to eleven p.m., earned from five to seven shillings per week, less ninepence for cotton and two and sixpence for the hire of her sewing-machine. Another (a shirt-finisher) stated that, after working hard all day, she could not earn more than fourpence-halfpenny.

But even this is not the worst paid work there is. Button-hole workers, who have to work neat holes five-eighths of an inch long, are paid at the rate of twopence-three-farthings per gross. A lady, speaking at an East-End meeting the other day, quoted the case of a woman known to herself, who is a widow and has children to support. She makes ulsters, and is paid threepence each for making them. She and her children were nearly starving—so nearly, that when some scraps of meat were given her, she said that if she were to leave them in the children's way they would fight for them.

Now, I am here to say that such women are in a worse condition of slavery than any likely to be enforced by a slave-holder, to whose interest it is that his slave should not die. Can you wonder that they say to us:

> 'Oh, to be a slave
> Along with the barbarous Turk,
> Where woman has never a soul to save,
> If this be Christian work'?

Can you wonder if such women take to vice and crime? I tell you that vice and crime cannot be a much greater curse than such conditions of life and labour. I do not wonder that the women of the submerged tenth turn out badly; the only wonder is that there is one pure soul among them—one who wears the white flower of a blameless life.

The question at once arises, What can be done? There is another question that must be answered first, and that is, What has brought about this state of things? I think the answer to that question will be found in the word Competition. First, competition among employers, who are for ever cutting each other down in prices for the sake of obtaining trade. The competition of those who want to live on their profits is aggravated by the competition of those who do not need to make profits, because they are supported from outside sources. And thus the man who must make a profit in order to live has to grind down his employés, and secure his profit by what he can save out of their wages.

Then, too, there is competition amongst the labouring classes themselves. If a woman or a man says to an employer, 'No; I will not work for a reduced wage,' either is met by the stereotyped reply: 'If you do not like it, you can go; there are plenty who will.' That is really the root of the evil—there are plenty who will. Low wages prevail, because the worker consents to accept them, and because no worker who stands alone can refuse them. The isolated worker must take what is offered or go without work; and to go without work means speedy starvation; to accept it at the lowest possible rate means a slower starvation, and every woman or man would rather of the two accept that.

And now comes the question, What is to be done? I assert, after a good deal of reflection, that charity—and I mean by that doles of money—is useless. To supplement ill-paid labour with doles is to endow a wrong system, and to support a pernicious principle. There are employers now who say, 'Oh yes, we only pay five or six shillings a week, but they don't depend on it: they are *helped* in various ways.'

Charitable donations to able-bodied men and women can only be, in effect, a rate in aid of wages, and therefore in the end a force towards the reduction of wages.

One thing we can do: we can help to create and to support a powerful public sentiment that shall demand honest pay for honest work. We can demand that the den of the sweater shall be closed. We can demand of the merchant or the manufacturers of whom we buy the necessaries of life that in their production men and women shall have received just wages. We can demand, by voice and pen, and by the still more powerful weapon, the money that we spend, that the producer shall be justly rewarded for his work.

Can you bear, sir, to think that the shirt you wear was made for the miserable sum of three-halfpence?

> 'Oh, men, with sisters dear!
> Oh, men, with mothers and wives!
> It is not linen you're wearing out,
> But human creatures' lives!'

It can never be right, never be fair, never be Christian, that facts should warrant such a song as this:

> 'There are ninety and nine that live and die
> In want and hunger and cold,
> That one may revel in luxury,
> And be wrapped in its silken fold:
> The ninety and nine in hovels bare,
> The one in a palace with riches rare.

> 'They toil in the fields do the ninety and nine,
>   For the fruitage of Mother Earth;
> They dig and they delve in the dusky mine,
>   And riches untold bring forth;
> But the wealth released by their sturdy blows
> To the coffers of one for ever flows.
>
> 'The sweat of their brows makes the wilderness bloom,
>   And the forest before them falls;
> Their labour builded our thousand homes,
>   And our cities with lordly halls;
> But the ninety and nine have empty hands,
> And one owns cities and homes and lands.'*

It can never be right that working-men and women should be taught to sing these words as a just description of their lot:

> 'We plough and sow, we're so very, very low,
>   That we delve in the dirty clay,
> Till we bless the plain with the golden grain,
>   And the vale with the fragrant hay;
> Our place we know—we're so very, very low—
>   'Tis down at the landlord's feet;
> We're not too low the grain to grow,
>   But too low the bread to eat.
>
> 'Down, down we go—we're so very, very low—
>   To the hell of the deep-sunk mines;
> But we gather the proudest gems that glow
>   When the brow of the despot shines;
> And whene'er he lacks upon our backs
>   Fresh loads he deigns to lay;
> We're far too low to veto the tax,
>   But not too low to pay.
>
> 'We're low, we're low—we're very, very low—
>   Yet from our fingers glide
> The silken flow and the robes that glow
>   Round the limbs of the sons of pride;

---

* From 'Anti-Poverty Songs.'

> And what we get and what we give
> We know, and we know our share;
> We're not too low the cloth to weave,
> But too low the cloth to wear.'*

That this is an exaggeration of the truth I quite believe, but that there is any truth in it at all is a terrible comment on our Christianity and on our sense of fairness. Whoever makes or produces a necessary of life or a luxury ought to be rewarded in a measure sufficient to meet all legitimate wants. 'Thou shalt not muzzle the ox that treadeth out the corn.'

For the labourers themselves I see no alternative, in the present state of things, to combination. I am not here to champion all the principles connected with Trades Unionism. Trades Unions have their evils, but I am perfectly convinced that those evils, great as they are, are as nothing compared with the gigantic tyrannies, injustices and inequalities by which the labourer has been oppressed. In demanding their rights the toilers may rush to extremes—they are rushing to extremes, mad extremes, some of them—but still their redemption lies in combination. It must be ours to see that tyranny does not exchange places; that the scourge which the capitalist once held does not pass into the hands of the labourer.

2. The other principle which I should like to inculcate is a recognition of the unity of interest that exists between capital and labour.

This principle, carried into effect, means the allotting to

---

* From 'Anti-Poverty Songs.'

the labourer, or artist, or artizan, in addition to his normal wages, a portion of the net gains accruing from his labour. I know I shall be severely handled for advocating such a principle, but I am certain that it is based upon the triple foundation of justice, philanthropy, and self-interest. Justice, because the man who supplies the labour for the production of a thing has a direct interest in the value of the thing produced, and ought to be a sharer of the gain or loss accruing from it. Philanthropy, because it is the best form of helping men to help themselves. Self-interest, because it will result in closer ties between employer and employed, in better work, and in more cheerful service.

Rightly carried into effect, the principle allows the employer to considerably increase the earnings of his workpeople without suffering any—even the smallest—diminution in the amount of his own profit. Paradoxical as this theory may seem, when examined carefully it soon turns into a matter of fact. Consider the waste that goes on under the existing wage-system, under which the worker is not concerned whether the business pays or loses. If you put a man on time-wage, he dawdles over the job as long as the foreman will let him; put him on piece-wage, and he scamps the work as much as the foreman will let him. Workingmen, taking them in the lump, work, like their employers, not from love of their work, but from love of its pecuniary results.

If masters want their men to do more work and better work; to work not merely for wages, but for the credit of the business; if they want them to avoid involving them in unnecessary expense, they must make the interests of their employés identical with the interests of their business. It must be, to some degree at least, a joint-stock concern with a limited liability.

You may tell me that that is a bubble theory. My answer is that it has been tried with the most assuring success. The country which has adopted it the longest, and the most widely, is France. And there evidence of its success meets you at every turn. In Switzerland, in Germany, and in other European countries, the system is in operation with admirable results. In America the profit-sharing firms include some of the most successful and most respected names in the business world. In England it has been adopted by a few large firms, but not to any very wide extent. A manager of one of the largest firms adopting the principle writes: 'So far the results have been satisfactory. The employés take a more lively interest in their work than is the case when working merely for wages, and are much more economical of time and material. On our own part we get a better choice of hands, who become attached to the place, and who are concerned in its prosperity.'

On the moral side the results of the method would be equally beneficial. We all know how bitter is the feeling existing to-day between Capital and Labour. And one of the most powerful causes of this animosity is the opinion so strongly entertained that it is unjust that all profits derived from labour should go to the capitalist. The spontaneous concessions which the system would make to the legitimate claims of labour in every phase of industry would tend permanently to sweeten the relations between employer and employed, to convert the working-man from a dissatisfied, and often dishonest, drudge, into a contented, willing, zealous co-operator, no longer **feeling** himself a slave toiling to gratify the greed **of a taskmaster,** but a co-partner with his superior. And **thus the teachings** of **the Christ would** find some faint fulfilment: 'One is your Master . . . and all ye are brethren.'*

* **For some of** the facts and figures in this sermon I am indebted to articles in the *Fortnightly Review*, vol. xlvi., p. 437.

The Sunday Question

IN THE LIGHT OF CHRISTIAN ETHICS.

ST. MATTHEW xii. 11, 12.

'And **He** said unto them, What man shall there be among you that shall have one sheep, and if it fall into a pit on the Sabbath day, will **he not lay hold of it,** and lift it out? How much then is a man better than a sheep? Wherefore it is lawful to do well on the Sabbath days.'

THE SUNDAY QUESTION

IN THE LIGHT OF CHRISTIAN ETHICS.

CITIZEN-SUNDAY has been instituted for the avowed object of seeking to impress upon the citizens of London the duties that arise out of their citizenship—duties to themselves and to one another.

In their appeal to the clergy and to ministers of all denominations to observe the day, the committee justly say: 'The very vastness of London benumbs our sense of its unity, and of the imperative necessity of corporate and concentrated action for its welfare. We cannot apprehend or fix our individual relation to it. The responsibilities that we are incurring moment by moment are so widely dissipated that they slip out of our sight. Each one of us is lost amid the crowd, and our public obligations lose themselves with us. Nothing can correct this defalcation of conscience but a large and organized rally of our total force of social energy. Our reason, imagination, heart and will, must all be touched by the heat of a universal endeavour. They must be roused from their apathy by a public challenge to face the tremendous charge laid upon them in all its fulness, its coherence, its seriousness, its terrible importunity.'

With that statement I cordially and entirely agree. We, the Church, the great body of citizens who name the name of the Christ the Son of Man, the Great Worker for men, the Divine Philanthropist—we at least must rise to our duties, and must heed with a determined will the importunate pleadings of our fellows for better surroundings, purer conditions of life, and fairer prospects for the attaining of even humble ideals. A thousand questions press themselves upon us, and wait in stately silence for our answer. Let us face them, and then by our noblest energies rid our consciences of the stain of indolence and unconcern.

I will not trouble you with a long list of the questions with which we should concern ourselves. I am going to confine my remarks to one question only, and that one of paramount importance—the Sunday question.

And I want first to say that in my opinion Sunday is one of the darkest blots on the face of our fair city. The way in which it is spent by the great masses of our fellow-citizens suggests nothing to my mind but ineffable sadness. I do not refer to the way in which the upper and middle classes spend their Sunday — with their church parade, their fashionable strolls, their afternoon receptions, their evening wine-parties. All that is stupidly inane in the upper classes, as the extra feeding, sleeping, and vicious idleness of the middle classes are unworthy alike of the day and its observer. What I have to say is mainly in reference to what is called—miscalled, no doubt, in many cases—the working class, that is, the vastly predominant class of this London of ours.

You know, because sneering newspapers and pessimistic

journalists are always telling you, that ninety-nine hundredths of this class do not observe Sunday in a religious way: that is, they do not go to places of worship. They are not careful, however, to tell you how they do observe it. Their object is to have a cheap sneer at religion, and not to awaken sympathy for the working classes. If only one in a hundred goes to church, where do the ninety and nine go? There is one sad, comprehensive, condemning answer, which embraces more than fifty per cent. of the men—the public-house! That is their church, their recreation-room, their holiday resort. They repair thither at the earliest opportunity: hang about the street-corners waiting till the restricted hours have passed, and then they enter and remain—many of them till closing time, most of them longer than is consistent with soberness.

It is easy enough to call them boozers, drunkards, Sabbath-breakers, and the like. Any fool can call a mad dog names. Have we ever thought of the reason for all this? Why does the working man spend his Sunday in the public-house, or in some low club that has no restricted hours and exists simply for the pleasures of drink?

It is obvious that he must spend his Sunday somewhere. Religion and custom combined have told him that Sunday is a day of rest, a holiday. He must not go to his workshop; he must not handle his tools, or ply his trade. So far, so good; for that at least let God be thanked. In these days of stress and toil it is a blessed thing to have coming once a week, breaking in upon life's hurly-burly, the calm, the rest, the relaxation of the Sabbath. In ideal the thought is glorious—nothing more so in our national life. Where the misery comes in is in the observance. And I do not hesitate to say that as it is observed by the majority of the people it is a curse rather than a blessing.

Let us try, then, to get at the root of the matter; let us see what, in the economy of life, the day might be.

First, let us be clear as to whence, and for what objects, we get our Sabbath. I need not, of course, tell you that the day has its origin in the Mosaic law. It was given by Moses to the Israelites at a very early period of their history, partly as a sign between God and them, thus marking them off from all other nations by its observance, and partly as commemorating their deliverance from Egypt. In the fourth commandment, as we use it to-day in the Decalogue, the reason given for observing the day is that on the seventh day God rested from His creative work; that He hallowed the seventh day, and made it holy for all time. Whereas, if you turn to the book Deuteronomy you will find Moses urging the observance of the Sabbath for another reason. He says: 'Keep the Sabbath-day to sanctify it. . . . And remember that thou wast a servant in the land of Egypt, and that the Lord thy God brought thee out thence through a mighty hand and by a stretched out arm: *therefore* the Lord thy God commanded thee to keep the Sabbath-day.' But at the bottom lay the broader, more humanitarian reason—man's need for *rest*. The day was a recognition of the fact that man is so constituted that he must have regular periodical cessation from toil.

Our Lord tells us that 'the Sabbath was made for man.' Because man is what he is, therefore the Sabbath was ordained. Moses seized upon the fact to impress upon a people naturally inclined to idolatry and to a materialistic form of religion the duty of consecrating a fixed portion of their time to Jehovah. Starting at the bottom that the day was a day of rest, based on the fact that God rested, and that hence He hallowed rest as well as toil, he rose to the higher fact that man, being a spiritual creature, might consecrate the day to God in holy worship. And so rigidly did he fence around this conception of one day in seven being given to God, that no fire was permitted to be made, on pain of death; no food was to be prepared, nor the smallest feature of trade tolerated. For gathering a few sticks on the Sabbath a man was arraigned before the congregation and sentenced to death. That was the Mosaic spirit, which was fostered and cherished by the Jewish Church till the time of our Lord. The Judaistic party out-Mosesed Moses in the severity which they imposed upon the Sabbatic rest. Not only would they neither do nor countenance work of any kind in themselves, but they even went so far as to debate whether it was not a violation of the Sabbath if on the first day of the week they ate an egg laid by a hen on the seventh day of the week.

But what said the Christ to this conception of the day of rest? From the first He ignored it as a thing alien to the Divine purpose. Many of His works of mercy He performed on the Sabbath, although He knew that in doing this He would shock and scandalize every religionist of His time. He allowed His disciples to act in utter violation of Jewish law. He boldly declared that the Sabbath was instituted, not for man's privation, but for man's good. It was a day for beneficence, not for asceticism. He protested against the idea that works of mercy, and deeds of love, and acts of helpfulness were desecrations of the day, or of its Author.

We know what ground His followers took. We know how little by little the Jewish Sabbath dropped out of their lives altogether, and how in its place they established a new rest-day, viz., the first day of the week, because it was their Lord's day—the day on which He rose triumphant over death. We know that from that time to the present all Christians have observed the first day.

Now I ask, By what logic are you going to retain the restrictions of the Mosaic Sabbath while you play fast and loose with the day itself? For remember that the very commandment which says, 'In it thou shalt do no manner of work,' also says, 'The *seventh* day is the Sabbath of the Lord thy God.' If, on the other hand, you contend—as I do most sincerely—that the fourth commandment is not binding on these points, you will see that it is not the enactment itself that is sacred, but the facts underlying it, viz., man's need of rest, and the Divine will that He should consecrate it to highest ends. The Pharisees of Christ's time maintained that the necessities of man's nature must yield to the letter of a legal enactment; Christ taught that the letter of the enactment must yield to man's necessities. The day itself is nothing; what lies behind it is everything. 'One man esteemeth one day above another,' writes St. Paul; 'another esteemeth every day alike.' And he simply adds: 'Let every man be fully persuaded in his own mind,' as though he would say, It matters little which day you observe, so long as you observe one, and keep before you the Divine principle implied.

And yet, with the words and deeds of Jesus before us, with the teachings of His blessed Apostles in our minds, is it not strange that for three centuries we have been trammelled with the spirit of Judaism? 'The Sabbath was made for man,' said the Master. 'Yes,' said our Puritan forefathers, 'to scathe him, scourge him, deprive him, humble him, afflict him.' They would have the old rigidity of the Jewish Sabbath, and, while changing the day that God ordained, they strictly kept the letter of the enactment in regard to work. And, what is worse, they not only refused to enjoy the rest-day themselves, but they determined that no one else should enjoy it. It was essentially a day in which men were made to afflict their souls.

Who that has reached middle-life does not remember the dreary Sabbaths of his youth? Games of every kind were forbidden; music, save some dreary hymn-tune, was silenced; reading was inadmissible, unless the reader was content with his Bible, Prayer-Book, or some other religious work. A kind of unnatural silence reigned in the house, and everywhere. Gloom and lugubriousness were predominant.

I want to assert—and with all the emphasis of which I am capable—that that is not the Christ-spirit. Like a great many other things in Puritanism, it is a perversion of what is, and might be made for everyone, a glorious institution. I have said that God gives us the day of rest because it is a necessity. The rest was jealously guarded by Moses because amongst a nomadic people rigidity of rule had to be maintained. Jesus our Lord acknowledged the Divineness of the rest-day, but He would have none of its restrictions. So far as we can learn, He did precisely on the Sabbath that which He did every other day. The Jewish idea was separateness; His was permeation. The Jew hedged around one day from all unhallowed associations;

He would make all days holy. The Jew reserved sanctity for certain offices and certain places; He saturated all life with God, and flooded all earth with heaven.

Well, how does this bear upon the question which we have set ourselves to consider here? Let us see. We acknowledge the Divineness of the institution of the Sabbath as meeting a physical, moral, and spiritual necessity in man. We say that it is a Divine law that every man should rest from his ordinary work one day in seven. We acknowledge the fitness of the first day of the week for that rest, because of its hallowed associations. We believe that the early Christians acted perfectly within their right, not only in rejecting the rigour of the Jewish Sabbath, but in changing the day. But what have we to say of the day? How should it be spent? and in what way? If we reject the Puritan notion, what have we to advocate in its stead? What are we to say to those teeming thousands of toilers who are cut off from their work, and must spend the day somehow, somewhere? Of course, the ideal is the principles that underlay the Puritan Sabbath—consecration and worship. We should like to see all the sons and daughters of toil presenting themselves before the Lord in holy worship; we should like to hear their voices uplifted in songs of thanksgiving. That is the ideal. And we are sure that the ideal, if realized, would make for the uplifting of mankind. But while man is what he is, the realization is impossible. Men won't give the day to God because God is not realized by them: He is not a part of their lives in any way. Their capacities for God lie dormant. And you might just as well tell a lot of blind people to go to the National Gallery, or a number of deaf people to go to a classical concert, as tell them to go to church. More's the pity, I know, but the fact remains: church means nothing to them. What have they left? Their homes and the public-house. If you go to their homes, you will find nothing there to induce a man to spend his Sabbath in them; you will find many things—dirt, dreariness, squalor—to send a man out of them. The homes of some of the working-men of England are a disgrace to them, and hence to us. They have nothing left, then, but the street and the public-house; and what that means to them anyone with eyes to see may soon learn: it means the degradation of their manhood, the bartering away of their self-respect, the ruining of the temple of God, the blighting of their lives, and the suicide of their better natures. That is what it means.

'Shut the public-houses,' say some. Well, I have no objection to that if you do it on the principle that the publican should not be privileged beyond others in his opportunities for plying his trade. But I do object to it if you do it on the ground that the working-man shall have no place of resort; that he shall be driven out to the streets or back to his bed. You will never make men righteous by law; nor will you ever increase man's nobility by removing temptation out of his way. What, then, would I do? I would give them other opportunities, and such opportunities as should be powerful rivals to the public-house—opportunities that should appeal to the better nature in them, and woo and win them to loftier ideals, nobler manners, purer conduct.

I would make access to the country easy on Sunday; I would open every museum and art gallery that our cities possess; I would have music in our parks and public squares and halls; I would have lectures on science, on art, on manufacture, on the thousand and one problems of life. I would make the day a festal day, with one broad banner stretched across it from dawn till midnight, and on the banner inscribed one word—'Love.' Then, not only would the religionist sing,

> 'Bright days! we need you in a world like this.
> Be brighter still! Ye cannot be too bright.
> The world's six days of vanity and toil
> Would, but for you, oppress us with their might.
>
> 'Bright days! in you heaven cometh nearer earth;
> And earth more fully breathes the balm of heaven;
> The stillness of your air infuses calm;
> Fairest and sweetest of the weekly seven!
>
> 'Bright days! abide with us; we need ye still.
> Ye are the ever-gushing wells of time;
> Ye are the open casements where we hear
> The distant notes of heaven's descending chime':

the poor, the down-trodden, the weary, the sinful, and the great mass of toilers would join in the song.

I will attempt very briefly to meet some objections that have been raised to this free way of spending Sunday.

1. There is the puritanical religionist's objection that it is a desecration of the day.

The Lord's words are an answer to that: 'What man shall there be that shall have one sheep, and if it fall into a pit on the Sabbath-day, will he not lay hold of it, and pull it out? How much, then, is a man better than a sheep?' Our brother men have fallen into the pit—the pit of sensualism, of dull, dreary, unheavenly materialism, and anything that will help to get them out is lawful. 'The Sabbath was made for man.'

2. The next objection is that it entails a vast amount of labour for those who are already sufficiently hard-worked; that it would take away the Sabbath from a great number who need its rest equally with other toilers. True; but Sunday is not the only day in the week on which rest can be found. Where men have to work at night they sleep during the day, and accommodate themselves to the arrangement. It would be perfectly easy to secure for those who work on Sunday a rest-day during the week, and to provide for them on that day all the privileges of worship and relaxation that others enjoy on the Sunday. The justice of the nation ought to secure for every man one day of absolute respite from accustomed toil in every seven.

3. Another objection is that it would empty our churches. So much the more shame on the Church if, with her music her liturgies, her vast talents for educating, informing, and gratifying man's highest tastes, her wealth, and her Divine mission, she can't compete with museums and art galleries. I think it would have the opposite effect. All beauty tends Godwards; to draw men away from their low surroundings, and from their lower selves, is to bring them heavenward. I have implicit faith in all refining influences: they are among the regenerating forces of the world.

4. Another objection is the economical objection. It would cost so much. Yes, it would be expensive; but we

had better spend our money on that than on beer and horse-racing. We spend nearly two hundred million pounds for these things every year; a tenth of that spent on our Sundays would turn them into heavenly days, crowded with heavenly messages. The nation can afford to do it; the man in the pit must be lifted up.

I commend these thoughts to you. Think generously of them; think charitably. If you do not accept my conclusions, give me credit for sincerity of motive, and for the desire to serve alike my fellows and my God. The Pharisees called our blessed Lord a Sabbath-breaker. 'They kept the law of the Sabbath, but they broke the law of love.' They strained out a gnat, and yet swallowed a camel. Take heed, lest in your over-zeal for the externals of religion you copy them, and not the Christ. Make the Sabbath a delight. Say,

> 'Thou art a day of mirth;
> And where the week-days trail on ground,
> Thy flight is higher, as thy birth:
> O let me take thee at the bound,
> Leaping with thee from seven to seven,
> Till that we both, being toss'd from earth,
>   Fly hand in hand to heaven.'

Parental Duties

IN THE LIGHT OF CHRISTIAN ETHICS.

1 SAMUEL ii. 19.

'His mother made him a little coat.'

ST. MATTHEW xviii. 10.

'Take heed that ye despise not one of these little ones.'

PARENTAL DUTIES

IN THE LIGHT OF CHRISTIAN ETHICS.

AT the time that judges ruled in Israel, and before the days of Judaic monarchy, there lived at Ramathaim-Zophim—a place the precise locality of which cannot now be determined—one Elkanah, who, in all probability, was a Levite. From the little that the historic narrative tells us about him, we gather that he was a man of good, liberal nature, free and happy in his ways, kind and open-handed in his home, and loving to his wives—for he had two—but especially tender to the one whom he loved with the greater affection.

It may be noted that the historian, while freely recording the fact of his having more than one wife, does not mention it as a blameworthy or reprehensible thing. No comment whatever is made; no hint that it was either immoral or irreligious. It may have been then, as it is with the Samaritans to this day, that, one of his wives being childless, social usage permitted marriage with another.

In Elkanah's home there were two wives, but by no means two kindred souls. One was bitter in spirit, and heart-weary at seeing the happy motherhood of the other;

and the other, jealous because of the diversion of her husband's greatest love to the childless one, made her own blessing of children a perpetual taunt and irritation to the disconsolate Hannah. For it seems that Elkanah's devoted love was lavished on the childless wife, and so life was made bitter to each by two distinct and different causes.

The yearly act of worship, in which all the family went up to Shiloh, full-handed with offerings to the Lord from Elkanah's liberality, and joyful, as those should be who went up to keep the Feast of Tabernacles, came as an annual climax to Hannah's grief. At one of these annual visits, feeling in the bitterness of her soul that she could endure her childlessness no longer, we are told that she stood before the Lord, and prayed, and wept sore: 'And she vowed a vow unto the Lord, and said, O Lord of hosts, if Thou wilt indeed look on the affliction of Thine handmaid, and remember me, and not forget Thine handmaid, but wilt give unto Thine handmaid a man child, then I will give him unto the Lord all the days of his life.'

And standing there with tears of suppliance on her cheeks, and the sobs of a bruised and breaking heart on her lips, a voice spake to her, saying, 'Go in peace.' The desire of her heart was granted Elkanah's household was brightened with the presence of a child from the wife whom he loved. And when next they went to Shiloh it was not with sadness ; when next Hannah prayed in the tabernacle it was not silently, nor with a bitter heart and tearfulness, but with triumphant praise, and a song that irresistibly carries on the heart to the hymn that magnified the Lord as it poured forth from the soul of the Mother of Jesus.

How overflowing was Hannah's joy ! How she welcomed

little Samuel as a direct gift from God in answer to her prayer! And her joy did not shut the remembrance of her vow out of her heart. With a grateful heart she performed her wonted pilgrimage, but with a new gift in her hand. God's gift was to be given back to Him at His own shrine. As she handed him to the aged Eli, she said: 'For this child I prayed, and the Lord hath given me my petition which I asked of Him, therefore have I lent him to the Lord. As long as he liveth he shall be lent to the Lord.' And hence Samuel found his home in the tabernacle of the Lord's house. And, as he grew, he 'ministered before the Lord, being a child girded with a linen ephod. Moreover, his mother made him a little coat, and brought it to him from year to year when she came with Elkanah to offer the yearly sacrifice.' What the coat was we are unable to say, but whatever its shape or texture, it must have been a rich and becoming garment that was made for a child that had been lent unto the Lord.

But why have I chosen this as a text? Because it brings before us a mother who recognised the solemn responsibilities of motherhood; a mother who took in the twofold possibilities of her child's life: the spiritual and the physical—the psychical and the animal. As a spiritual entity, she lent him to the Lord; as a physical being with physical wants, she made him a little coat.

It is of this twofold nature of the duties of parents that I want to speak: our duties in relation to our children as physical beings, and our duties in relation to them as moral and spiritual beings. It is an infinitely solemn thing to be a parent. Every child born into the world is a bundle of tremendous responsibilities, and whether it shall come forth into life, its heart attuned to the eternal harmonies, and after a life of usefulness on earth go to a life of joy and bliss in the immortal sphere, or whether across it shall jar eternal discords, and after a life of wrong-doing on earth it shall go off into impenetrable darkness, is much more determined by the fulfilment or the neglect of parental duties than we are wont to recognise.

1. I will speak of parental duties as they affect the physical natures of children.

(*a*) And, first of all, I want to emphasize this fact, with all the earnestness born of a profound conviction, that no one has a right to become a parent who is not prepared to fulfil all the obligations that are incumbent upon parents.

I am oftentimes perfectly astounded at the careless, irresponsible way in which the procreation of children is regarded. Men and women whose means barely suffice to keep bodies and souls together go on having children as though they were breeding animals which could be sold when the stock proved larger than the capacities of the larder. It is a sin against society, it is a sin against posterity, to bring children into the world with no prospect of being able to bring them up into manhood or womanhood without privation; as, indeed, it is a greater sin still to become parents when in the very act of procreation you give to your children germs of disease or vice that will be a curse to them so long as they breathe the breath of life.

It is idle and impious to say that God never sends mouths without sending food to fill them. God has placed in your hands the power of procreation, and if you multiply offspring while your poverty or your misfortune is a curse to you, you might as well babble the heathen gibberish of Kampschatka, as pray that God would feed and clothe your children. He expects us to act in accordance with His laws, social as well as moral; and to defy those laws and then pray that God will intervene is not only 'a far cry to heaven,' but an insult to the eternal majesty of the Lawgiver.

God has placed it within the power of every man and woman to determine whether they will be parents or not: it is only mad folly or base sensualism which says these things are outside our control. They are absolutely and completely within the control of everyone, and you have no right to choose to be a parent, or indulge the faculties that lead to parenthood, unless you are prepared to realize that upon your head the eternal responsibilities of parenthood rest. How many parents could say with Hannah, ' For this child I prayed '? Where there is one who can say so, there are many who regard every addition to the family as an unmitigated nuisance.

(*b*) But to proceed with parental duties to children. Having begotten them, it is your parts and duties to see that the faculties, functions and capacities of their nature are met, trained, exercised to the utmost limits of your powers.

I do not think that parents ever half sufficiently consider their responsibility in regard to the perfecting of the physical nature of their children. Not only should every possible care be exercised in procreation, so as not to transmit to offspring anything that will be a curse or an impediment to them, but, having begotten them, it is our never-ceasing duty to guard, direct, control and help them against every possible deformity and imperfection. Oh, how many of us suffer, not only from our parents' follies and sins before they were parents, but from their deliberate neglect after that we became their charge!

Do not think it a thing beneath your notice to see that even your children's teeth grow regularly, that they learn to carry themselves without stooping, that their habits of eating and drinking, as well as the things they eat and drink, are such as conduce to their health and general well-being. Small things have often mighty issues. Always remember two things in respect to your children: first, that their bodies were intended to be God's temple. See, therefore, that from the first they form habits of cleanliness, neatness, order. Point out to them the marvellous skill and wisdom displayed in their creation. Teach them reverence for their bodies as a whole, and for certain functions that lie at the very base of life in particular, as all lying within the goodwill and purpose of God. Secondly, remember that they in turn are to become progenitors; that when the grass will be growing green on your grave they will be men and women with children and grand-children flitting about the avenues of their life. A defect or a deformity caused by your neglect will transmit itself to posterity, and you will thus become the parent of ills that never come within the scope of God's purpose.

Moreover, I think it to be the duty of all parents to give their children the benefit of their experience in all the things that pertain to them in their relation to the opposite sexes. Tens of thousands have been led to perdition for want of a few words of warning or of explanation from those to whom they had the right to look as much for education in those matters, as in how to use their legs when they were learning to walk. Is it not surprising that the very things that most affect our happiness or misery, the things that, more than any others, go to the making or the marring of the whole of life, are the things that most parents never talk to their children about? I would have every mother realize that it is as much her duty to teach her daughter the meaning and the mystery of all the wondrous functions of her budding womanhood as to teach her to pray. I would have every father realize that it is his duty to teach his son the secrets of purity and the right government of his passions, as much as to teach him to read or to write. And, as parents, you must do it yourselves; do it seriously, do it earnestly, do it, if you will, on your knees before God; but you *must* do it. It doesn't come within the scope of what is called scholastic education; it doesn't lie within the province of the pulpit: it is your special province, and on your rightful performance of the duty the fate of your child may hang. What St. Paul wrote to Timothy, ' Keep thyself pure,' you ought to write on all the outgoings and incomings of your child's life. It is abhorrent pruriency that prevents the discussion of these things between parents and children. The young are naturally curious, and if you do not tell them they will inquire about these things of others probably as ignorant as themselves, and that often means the opening of the floodgates through which streams of vice flow.

(*c*) Again, I think it a duty of parents to manifest interest in all that concerns the life of their children.

'There is only one thing that I love Martin Luther for, and that is, not his theses on the doors of the Wittenberg church, wherein he defied the Pope—I don't care an old button about those theses—but I love him because he played at trundling hoops with his children. I am very fond of Charles Kingsley the novelist, but Charles Kingsley scrambling sweets on the lawn at Eversley, or writing that delightful story, 'The Water Babies,' purely for the amusement of his own children, is more admirable still. But the Luthers and Kingsleys are not by any means typical fathers; they are, I fear, very rare exceptions. If in many cases the advent of another baby is regarded as a nuisance, in quite as many cases are the children in their growing years nuisances. How many times have parents been heard to say: 'I could do this, that, or the other, but for the brats!' How many fathers are there who insist that the children shall all be got off to bed before they come home for their evening meal! Fathers they may be, but they are not men in the noblest sense of that word.

There is something radically wrong where a child is ever a nuisance, no matter what its faults or failings. A father is infinitely more a man when he buys toys for his children, than when he spends his money on sumptuous mid-day meals, or on wine and cigars. The meanness which talks of children being a great drain on one's resources, and of compelling one to economize, greatly to one's discomfort, finds no place in perfect parenthood, which is built upon altruism and glorified by love. St. Paul emphasizes it when he says: 'Children ought not to lay by for their parents, but parents for their children.'

2. I turn now to the moral and spiritual aspect of parental duties.

And I would impress you with this fact, that your duties to your child as a moral and spiritual being are equal to, or even more important than, your duties to him as a physical being. In both cases the duties begin at the cradle. As an actor, conscious and voluntary, a child is nothing; a puppy, a kitten, a lamb is endowed with as many qualities as a newborn child—except in the matter of potentialities. Where the child transcends the animal is in the fact that the animal will be bound to the realm and sphere of the animal world for ever; it will affect nothing outside the merely animal; whereas a child has in it germs of a life and destiny which may shape or shake empires, which may influence the whole world of men for time and for eternity. And in this matter the responsibilities of parenthood are so great, because parents impress their children as no others can impress them, and because they impart to them influences which will go with them into life, into death, into eternity.

If you want your son to grow up a noble-minded man, do not let him be impressed with the fact that you regard eating and drinking and the gratification of the senses as the Alpha and Omega of existence; let him learn from you that altruism is the secret source of all the real happiness, and the basis of the loftiest nobility, that are known to this life. If you want your daughter to grow up to be a queenly woman, do not let her see that your own and her dress are the A and the Z of your entire planning. How can a child be taught the grand lessons of self-denial, frugality, humility, and spiritual-mindedness when you smother it with the artificial trappings of pride and extravagance? Do not transform an immortal being into a doll-baby, or give it the idea that the realization of the latest fashion-plate is the ideal of life.

Give your child a shilling to spend at toyshops, or in those pernicious things, 'sweets,' and a half-penny for the offertory when it comes to church, and you teach that child that self-indulgence is twenty-four times as important as Christian charity and sacrifice to God.

I think, too, that parents are not only in a great measure responsible for their children's dispositions, but also for their tempers. Always be scolding your children, and knocking one's head against the other, and if they turn out to be mild and sweet-tempered, it will be a miracle. There are a great many of us who can sympathize with Sydney Smith, who said that the clouds of his boyhood were never larger than a woman's hand, but that they usually ended in a squall. That is fatal to child-life.

If a child is handled harshly, or jerked into obedience, always found fault with, and never praised for doing his best, he will most probably turn out a sulky, obstinate, irritable creature. And yet that that kind of thing is constant in hundreds of households, one knows from observation. Here is a reported incident of what took place in one such: Mother, to her eldest child: 'Where is Bertha, and what is she doing?' Child: 'I don't know, mother.' Mother: 'Then go and find her, and tell her she mustn't!'

'She mustn't!' What a bugbear those words have been to many a child's life!

Do not think that the children are on the road to ruin because they make a racket. Noise is a sign of life, and is, in my opinion, one of the greatest aids to growth and health.

Do not talk disparagingly of your children in their presence, or be always scolding them as irremediable reprobates. Always be telling your daughter that she is the worst girl you ever knew, and do not be surprised if she turns out to be the worst woman you ever knew. Children are quick to observe, ready to catch and retain impressions. Every sentiment that looks into the eyes of a child looks back again out of the eyes in the form of character.

Remember, too, that they will think much more of what you do than of what you say. Some day in your boy's presence, in a hasty moment, you drop an oath. Quick as lightning it is out and gone. You say to yourself afterwards: 'I hope the boy won't take to swearing.' You need not hope; you have taught him, and he will do as you have done, and think it one of the signs of manliness because 'father does it.'

Again, children are very quick to detect the reality or the hypocrisy of your religion. It will not be enough that you teach them to pray: you must live your prayer. If they see you very devout in church, very attentive to the prayers, very glib in your recitation of the creed on Sunday, and yet on Monday see you practising positive deception, violating some principle which their unseared conscience pronounces right; if they hear you slandering and backbiting, and see that your temper is not under proper control, they will judge your religion at its proper worth, that is, a miserable sham. A child's conscience mirrors in its translucent depths the essential elements of the heavenly kingdom, and woe betide you if the elements reflected in your conduct and character do not in some measure answer to theirs! It was not without a meaning for all time that the Master once took a little child, and set him in the midst of the disciples as a type of the kingdom of heaven.

Be careful in talking of religion and religious things that you do not give false impressions. I cannot say what the majority of the children of to-day think of religion; I only know that the impression made on my mind when a boy was that religion was a very gloomy and sombre thing, and not at all in keeping with the exuberance of a child's spirits, or the abundant cheerfulness of a child's nature. I am afraid the impression is not dead yet. Sunday in many homes is a day of lugubriousness. All music, save some doleful hymn-tune, is silenced; mirth is checked or suppressed as out of keeping with the day; the tone of voice, the dress, the manners, are all Sabbatarian. And hence the one day in the week that children ought to love the best they love the least. A lugubrious Sabbath is a caricature of the holy day. 'Sunday books' are mostly monstrosities; all pure, helpful literature is as fit for Sunday as for week-days; all music is sacred that is not associated with vulgar words; all beauty, brightness, cheerfulness, are consistent with the Lord's Day. The Christian religion is not a dark angel bringing night-shadows under its wings, it is a bright angel dropping brightest benedictions on the hearts of men; and it is your duty to teach your children these things.

Teach them that God is interested in them; that He loves them, and that our sins grieve Him. Bring down to their minds in all the loveliness of His character, His meekness, His simplicity, the Ideal Man, Jesus our Lord.

Teach them that they may go to Him with their sorrows; that He is with them in their joys, and that He waits to present them in a glorious angelhood to His Father in heaven.

Thus treat them, thus teach them, and though you may leave them no riches, no property, you will leave them that which is infinitely preferable, the secret of God's peace, which shall make the memory of you an evangel, and the thought of you an angel of blessing.

The Animal World

IN THE LIGHT OF CHRISTIAN ETHICS.

St. Matthew x. 29.

'Are not two sparrows sold for a farthing? and one of them shall not fall on the ground without your Father.'

1 St. Peter iii. 8.

'Be pitiful.'

THE ANIMAL WORLD

IN THE LIGHT OF CHRISTIAN ETHICS.

IT has been laid at the door of the Christian religion—sometimes as a slur by the scoffer; sometimes as an indictment by the sceptic; sometimes as a matter of the deepest regret by Christians themselves—that the animal kingdom outside man finds no recognition in its creeds, its moral maxims, or its ethical dogmas; that animals are never mentioned, except as the servants of, or food for, the lord of creation.

Sir Edwin Arnold, in a most interesting essay on the question, 'Are Animals Moral?' says: 'All Christian peoples stand, for the most part, a sadly long way behind those of the East in their conduct to animals. Good Buddhists never intentionally take away life at all. The modern Hindoos of any good caste, borrowing from Buddha his noble regard for the right of everything to live, never touch meat as food, seldom even fish. . . . By a single decree of Mohammed the whole of Islam acts a thousand times more kindly to animals than Christendom.'

That is a statement which almost amounts to an indictment; and in so far as the practice of those who profess and call themselves Christians is concerned, I for one am bound to admit that it is a just indictment. But that the fault lies with the Author of Christianity, or the moral maxims of His religion, I indignantly and emphatically deny. It is due to the ignorance, the thoughtlessness, and the perverted tastes of Christians.

I want you to think of man's relation to the animal world, and then I will point out to you how the religion we profess bears upon our conduct to animals generally.

1. And first grasp this fact, that man and every living creature have a common origin.

I do not care what theories you hold as to Biogenesis; I do not care whether you follow Moses or Darwin in accounting for the phenomena of life upon earth—this is a fact which cannot be gainsaid, that man shares with every animal that lives the primal elements of life and the constituent elements of life. Life in germ form and in the embryonic stage is one and the same for a thousand varieties of animals, including man. In his most interesting work on 'Vertebrate Embryology,' Marshall states that 'All animals living, or that ever have lived, are united together by blood relationship of varying nearness or remoteness, and every animal now in existence has a pedigree stretching back, not merely for ten or a hundred generations, but through all geologic time since life first commenced on the earth.'

It is astonishing, too, what wondrous similarity exists between many of the organs and organic functions in man and those of other animals—the organs that perform the functions of secretion and excretion, of inhalation and exhalation; those that promote the digestion of food and the formation of blood-corpuscles; the various ducts and canals, nerve-centres and muscle-tissues—all have a striking likeness in man and beast. Speaking of ourselves, we say, in the language of the old Hebrew poet: 'For I am fearfully and wonderfully made'; but the smallest insect that spreads its gossamer wings under the glowing rays of the summer's sun equals, if it does not surpass, us in the fearfulness and wonderfulness of its creation. We think that man is the crown and glory of creation: in potentiality he may be; but there is evidence of as much creative skill, as much marvellous design, as much lavishness of endowment, as much delight in the work of the Creator's hands in the bee, the butterfly, the humming-bird, and the eagle, as in what Shakespeare calls 'the paragon of animals,' man. The denizens of the mighty depths of ocean, as well as those that skim and float and fly in the vaulted dome of heaven, vie with man in witnessing to the studious care displayed by God in the adaptation of faculty to function and function to environment. As far, too, as provision for their mere animal wants is concerned, it is as abundant for the brute as the man. 'He filleth all things living with plenteousness,' giving to all alike with an open hand, and with no sign of favouritism.

2. I want now to emphasize the fact that animals possess, along with man, though not in the same degree, the powers of volition for constructive, preservative, and pleasurable ends. Time was when men disputed that animals had minds; instinct was allowed them, but reason denied them. That disputation has now been removed

into the limbo of dead follies. We have come to discern—and that so clearly as to leave no room for doubt—that animals betray intelligence, and in many cases of a very marked and high degree; that they share with us many of the finer feelings and emotions; that they have memories; that they continually form progressive percepts; that they invent new means and methods of gratifying their faculties for enjoyment, and that, like man, they learn by experience. I am not going to carry this phase of the argument so far as to ignore the tremendous difference existing between the potentialities and attainments of human reason and those of the reason of the brutes. Man, according to Mr. Romanes, stands alone in 'the power of objectifying ideas, or of setting one state of mind before another state, and contemplating the relation between them.' He says: 'The power to think is—or, as I should prefer to state it, the power to think at all is—the power which is given by introspective reflection in the light of self-consciousness. . . . We have no evidence to show that any animal is capable of thus objectifying its own ideas; and therefore we have no evidence that any animal is capable of judgment.' This notwithstanding, there is in many animals a marvellous amount of sagacity, and of thoughtfulness manifested in prevision and forecast, in courage and in self-sacrifice, in gratitude and in affection, even surpassing those things in man.

I might give you a long list of mental phenomena which man and brute share in common, though in varying degrees. But take those of the emotions only—fear, surprise, affection, pugnacity, curiosity, jealousy, anger, hatred, mirthfulness, sympathy, pride, resentment, grief, cruelty, benevolence, revenge, shame, regret, deceit, and in many cases an extreme sense and love of the beautiful—that some, or all of these, are common to a thousand forms of animal life nobody would deny.

I think, too, there is striking evidence that some animals possess faculties and powers which man does not possess, and that though we surpass them in reason, they surpass us in other potentialities which, if we knew their value, might make us envy the brute in its possession of them. I have seen a look in a dog's eye which gave me the impression that the dog knew, or had a sense of, something of which I was wholly ignorant. The ant, the bee, and the spider, from whatever motives they work, have certainly been man's teacher and precursor in constructive and adaptive methods of work. It is a humiliating thought to me that the bee and the spider can do what I cannot do, and that long before the human geometrician had formulated his laws, those laws existed in the brain of the tiny creature that wove its silken webs in the hedgerow. I should like to feel what the lark feels when it soars to heaven's gate and sings. Its song tells me that there is something thrilling in its tiny bosom to which my breast is a complete stranger.

> 'Teach us, sprite or bird,
>   What sweet thoughts are thine:
> I have never heard
>   Praise of love or wine
> That panted forth a flood of rapture so divine.
>
> 'Chorus Hymenæal
>   Or triumphal Chaunt,
> Matched with thine would be all
>   But an empty vaunt,
> A thing wherein we feel there is some hidden want.'

In face of these facts, who dares talk contemptuously of

the 'dumb animals,' of the 'lower creation,' and of the 'beasts that perish'? No animal is dumb to God: even the young lions, roaring after their prey, do seek their meat from Him. There is no such thing as 'lower orders of creation.' That which in our poor limited sight may seem the lowliest of all God's works, to Him may be the crown of His creative skill. And how know we that the brutes perish any more than man? Of ourselves we say, when overtaken by death, 'Then shall the dust return to the earth as it was, and the spirit shall return to God Who gave it.' The very science which has taught us the conservation of energy, and which thereby supports the Biblical doctrine of man's immortality, teaches us that in the economy of nature there is no such thing as destruction; dissolution, change, deformation, reformation, but no destruction. 'Nothing that once hath been, though ages roll between, and it be no more seen,' is lost. God has a place for every force that has taken to itself sphere or form, and it may be that over and above the many mansions which He has prepared for man in the great other world, He has made some provision for the other works of His hands. Science is certainly beginning to assert the doctrine of the immortality of all life, and from a rational point of view there is as much ground for believing in the immortality of the brute as of the man. 'It is the pitiless professors of materialism, who do not care how many gentle and helpless four-footed or four-handed beings they torture,' who can conceive for the brute nothing beyond an ephemeral existence which imposes no obligations on man. St. Paul speaks of the whole creation groaning and travailing in pain together, and certainly hints that that which shall come to man in the form of a higher destiny shall come also to every other work of God capable of realizing it. 'The earnest expectation of the creature waiteth for the manifestation of the sons of God.' I do not profess to take in the full meaning of this, and hence I do not dogmatize on a matter concerning which we must all necessarily be in the dark. But I have my own views and hopes on the question; and I, who admire all forms of life, and greatly love many, shall be disappointed if in the other life I do not find there some of the creatures to which I have become attached here.

3. I come now to the allegation that Christianity says nothing of man's duty to the animal world; that it is silent as to man's relationship with other forms of life.

According to the letter of the New Testament, this is mainly true, but according to the spirit of its teaching, it is absolutely and altogether false. If you seek for positive and direct commands against cruelty you will not find them. He Who said, ' Honour thy father and thy mother,' did not say, 'Be kind to, respect and reverence, all forms of life wherever you find them.' But we have something better, something infinitely higher than such a command as that: we have a God-life lived in God's world under purely human conditions; lived, too, to show us how every son of man should live; lived to leave us an example that we should follow in His steps. Look at that life, then, not alone in its relation to man, but in its relation to the world which was the scene of its activities; look at it in its relation to every creature and thing which formed its environment, and see if you can find anything but love, and pity, and gentleness, and sympathy, and respect, and reverence for everything God has made. Can you conceive of the lowly One of Nazareth, as He went about His Father's business, dropping benedictions upon the sordid, sorrowing, suffering, sinful lives of men—can you conceive of Him as even participating in an act of unkindness, of cruelty, of pain-giving to the very humblest of God's creatures? Did He not say that 'not a sparrow falleth on the ground without your Father'? Did He not unveil the world as impregnated with the Divine Presence, and all its phenomena as displays of the Divine wisdom and goodness? Did He not show how intimately God is connected with every form of life? Of the grass He said, God painted it; of the birds of the air, 'Your heavenly Father feedeth them.' I can think of Him as entering into the meaning and the mystery of the life and instincts and pleasures of the animal world; as seeing responsive elements existing between the Creator and the creature; as knowing how God takes in all life, and how in some way all life apprehends God.

Christianity means the copying of Christ; the reproduction of the tone, and temper, and emotions of His character in our characters. If He were really born in us, and reproduced in the whole of humanity, how differently would the relations existing between man and the other creatures of God be recognised! How changed would man's conceptions be of his duty towards his neighbours, the birds of the air and the beasts of the field, as well as his neighbour man!

Think, too, of the elements of the Christian religion as they were propounded by the Apostles of Christ, and see how they touch not only every phase of human life in its relations with human life, but how they impregnate character with a spirit that touches all things with reverence, and outpours itself on all things in love. 'The fruit of the spirit is love, joy, meekness, gentleness, long-suffering'; has that any bearing upon conduct in its relation to other forms of life? 'Be pitiful,' says St. Peter. Think you that he meant pity only for human woes and weaknesses and follies and sins? I think he meant for everything. The true Christman, in all his splendid, courageous, heroic elements of character, is one who is ever kind, and to whom cruelty is unknown.

> 'He prayeth well who loveth well
> Both man and bird and beast;
> He prayeth best who loveth best
> All things both great and small;
> For the dear Lord who loveth us
> He made and loveth all.'

Men once said that Christianity did not condemn, or even discountenance, slavery; and yet it was the spirit of Christianity firing the noblest souls of men that rose up to demand the abolition of slavery. And prate how men will about animals having no recognition in the Christian religion, that religion shall yet bring about for them higher consideration, more kindness, more thoughtfulness, yea, I would even say, as perfectly in keeping with the faith I hold, and more love from man.

The fact that, in our high state of civilization, we need such a society as that for the Prevention of Cruelty to Animals stands out as a sickening ulcer upon the fair face of our national life. It is a slur on our holy religion that not until recent years had we such a society as that which is now instituted—The Church Society for the Promotion of Kindness to Animals. Nor is the Church less Christian when she stands as the animal's friend than when she holds her synods for the settling of her theological dogmas.

It is essentially the mission of the Christian pulpit to tell men that they have no right to inflict needless pain upon any creature that shares with man life derived from God; and we must not hesitate to tell them so in words that they cannot misunderstand. We must say to Science, that in experimenting upon animals for the benefit of mankind she must deal tenderly, humanely, reverently, with even the humblest life she touches. We must tell Society that to encourage the slaughter of millions of the songsters of the air to provide the table with unnecessary delicacies is an outrage to Christian sentiment, and that to murder birds of gay plumage to decorate the attire of fashionable ladies is a wanton insult to the Creator. We must see that nowhere shall cruelty be practised for the pleasure or the gain of man. We must insist that where animals are killed for what man thinks to be necessary food, the process of killing shall be marked by all the kindness, care, and tenderness that is possible. Not to do this is, in my opinion, not to fulfil one of the highest phases of our mission to the world.

It is narrated of Mohammed that one day a young Meccan peasant brought to him two young pigeons which the feathered mother had followed all the way from the nest. 'See!' said Mohammed, 'she has more courage than the stoutest of my spearmen! She braves instant death for her younglings! Do you dream Allah created the heart of a dove like this, that you should carelessly spill the love and life forth from it at your fancy? I bid ye give back her couplet to that mother-bird; and henceforth never shall any true believer presume to slay a bird or a beast for food without first asking pardon from God and patience for the victim, repeating these words: *Bis'm Allah al Kerim* —In the Name of God the Compassionate.'* To the credit of Mohammedanism be it said that never since that day has any devout Mussulman tasted the flesh of bird or beast over which the *hallal* has not thus been pronounced. Is there not tenderness enough in our Christian sentiment to effect a similar thing? Are the followers of the gentle Christ to be less gentle than the Mussulman?

Christian men, Christian women, learn to be kind to every animal that would share with you in friendship the benisons of God. 'The mystery of their existence is profound; the long silence of their patience may cover solemn and terrible accusations which they will some day make against us before the Judgment-seat of the universal life!'

* Sir Edwin Arnold.

Hoops!

ECCLESIASTES ii. 14.

'The wise man's eyes are in his head; but the fool walketh in darkness.'

FOOLS!

ON hearing that the population of Great Britain and Ireland was, according to a census which had then just been taken, about thirty millions, Thomas Carlyle exclaimed, 'Thirty million people—mostly fools!' Probably, and the sage of Chelsea among the number. For the term 'fool' is a relative term, and in different mouths means wholly different things. There is no human standard of pronouncement by which we can apply it. You cannot measure a man's mind, or motive, or ideal, and then tabulate him wise or fool according to your measurement, as you can measure his stature by feet and inches and then pronounce him tall or short. There is something of the fool in every man—even the wisest; there is much of the fool in most men—even the best; there is all of the fool in many, though they be not so labelled or designated. If some angel from the other world were to come to earth, and label us according to our true merit, what an unfolding there would be! Ay, and what a hubbub when his work was done! How many of us who, in our conceit, think ourselves a bit above the common cut would be filled with surprise as we read our own label! What a sickening unfolding those four letters F O O L would be to many who think themselves more than ordinarily possessed of wisdom!

Let us observe, however, that the term is not applicable to inherent qualities, or the want of them, but to the use or abuse of such qualities as we may possess. It is not the largeness or smallness of the brain, the keenness or dulness of our mental capacities, the knowledge that we have stored up or passed by unheeded, that constitutes a man wise or foolish, philosopher or fool; no, but what we do with what we have. It is a question of ideal, motive, conduct, purpose, pursuit, and not of mental calibre or attainment. The man with little or no brain is an idiot; the man with the big brain who devotes its powers to unworthy ends, to the pursuing of low ideals, to the attaining of worthless objects, that man is a fool. The idiot is the man who has not; the fool is he who misuses what he has. And yet, bold as it may seem to say, the number of the latter surpasses the number of the former as the stars seen by the aid of the telescope surpass the number of those seen by the naked eye.

Fools! fools! How shall we speak of them? Where begin? Rich fools! poor fools! great fools! little fools! wise fools! ignorant fools! old fools! young fools! male fools! female fools! fools everywhere; thirty millions of people, mostly fools. Few idiots; fools in multitude! How shall we distinguish them? By what standard shall we judge them? For myself I decline to be judge or measurer. We may not act here as they act in detective tactics, where they 'set a thief to catch a thief.' As one conscious of what the label would be that the angel-visitant would affix to him I will not set up my own powers as capable of rightly judging others. To the law and the testimony we will go; to the highest rule of conduct known to mortals we will turn; by the brightest light in which men have seen light we will read. What saith the Bible? What saith God? Over and over again the voice of the Eternal hath spoken, and the listening ear has caught these words, 'Thou fool!' To whom were they spoken? To myriads, no doubt; but for convenience' sake we will classify them, and when classified we will take three as fairly representative of the fools of all time: 1. Fools in regard to religion. 2. Fools in regard to knowledge. 3. Fools in regard to worldly possessions.

1. Fools in regard to religion.

'The fool hath said in his heart, No God.' You must not adopt the reading of the Authorized Version or the Prayer-Book rendering of this statement. The original will not bear translating—'The fool hath said in his heart, There is no God.' All the wisdom of the ages were not equal to arriving at that conclusion. To be able to make such a statement as that, man must himself be possessed of some of the attributes which we ascribe to God. He must have measured all the heights above, and plumbed all the depths beneath; he must have peered into every secret hiding-place of the universe, and scanned all the infinite recesses of infinite space; he must have learnt how the things that are came to be; he must have seen the esoteric cause of every exoteric phenomenon; the riddle of life must be to him as an open vision, and the puzzle of death as a tale that is told; he must have been everywhere at the same moment, and seen everything at the same time, or how can he dare to say, 'There is no God'? An idiot, incapable of thought, powerless to reason, may say it; but a thinking mind, a reasoning judgment—never!

We do not need much philosophy to teach us that behind every effect there is a cause; that every consequent must have had a precedent; that every phenomenon is the result of action. The thinking minds of the world have come to the conclusion that the cause, the precedent, the active force, above, behind, and within all we see, and all that is, is God. Called by different names—'Jehovah, Jah, and Lord'—yet names that practically connote the same object, the Infinite, Eternal, Almighty Presence.

No; the fool's negation is not the negation of reason, but the negation of conduct. He does not say 'There is no God,' but he lives and acts as though there were none. He won't be affected by thoughts of God; he won't be trammelled by the everlasting *ought* that accompanies a recognition of God; he won't be distracted from his own selfish ends and purposes by any obligation that the thought of God imposes. He will go through life as though God were a myth, and His purposes dreams; he says in his heart, 'Be God what He may, He shall be nothing to me.' The Voice Eternal cries to all such, 'Thou fool!' and alas! the multitude to whom it cries! The world is thronged by men who do not doubt there is a God, who do not reason until they convince themselves that there is no God, who are not careful to ascertain what arguments there may be for or against the dogma that HE IS—the Eternal, EVERLASTING I AM; but who do not care a bent pin one way or the other; whose conduct is not affected, whose judgment is not touched, whose ideals are not governed, whose pursuits are not ordered by one single thought of Him, by one single concern about Him.

It may be doubted whether, impelled by reason, there is one single atheist in this world; it is absolutely certain that there are millions who are as indifferent to God as though He were a bronze monstrosity enshrined in a heathen temple; who give Him no more thought than they give to the inhabitants of the other planets that hang suspended in space. Practical atheists! Godless souls! Fools! No God! Life a babbling current over a stony bed; coming no whence, going no whither; with no recognition of the Divine 'I ought,' no care for the Divine 'I must!' Fools! Why? Because only in God is life realizable. Only in Him do we grasp the meaning and the mystery of life. Only in His light do the riddles find an answer, and the puzzles a solution. Only in Him is there satisfaction for those yearning capacities that disseverate and distinguish man from the brute. Only in seeking Him do we seek the absolute. Only in finding Him do we find rest.

> 'He lives who lives to God alone,
>   And all are dead beside :
> For other source than Him is none
>   Whence life can be supplied.
> For life within a narrow ring
>   Of giddy joys comprised
> Is falsely named, is no such thing,
>   But only DEATH disguised!'

Fools! We know them: the young man bent on sensuousness; the slave of his appetites, his passions, his basilar powers; given up to the pleasures of the table, the pleasures of the wine-cup, the pleasures of animalism, the greed of lust. No prayer to hallow his days; no white-winged angel to hallow his nights; no eye for the chariots of God sweeping through the heavens dropping benedictions; no thought of the Ineffable. Poor little shrivelled, atheistic soul! No God! No God!

One of such, and a typical one, visited Niagara in company with some kindred souls. As he stood above the raging cataract, and looked at it leaping, surging, dancing, laughing, throwing up here a pearly mist of gauzy glory, and there a rainbow of gorgeous hues, he put his little disc of glass to his eye and simpered: 'Neat; yes, very neat.' Turning to leave the stupendous scene, his eye caught the form of one of the females who had travelled with them, tricked out in colours that might make the rainbow spanning Niagara's mighty gorge hide itself in the mist. Her virtue was no greater than it should be; but as the eye-glassed youth saw her, he exclaimed: 'By Jove! isn't she magnificent!' Niagara was 'neat'; a woman in fashion's gaudy array—flesh and blood that appealed to the brute in him—was 'magnificent.' I know that young man. I see him in every West-End club, and at every ball. He stares at me out of every box in the theatre. I meet him in every thoroughfare. I hear his guffaw in every wine bar! Faultlessly dressed; able to carry his walking-stick and umbrella in the approved fashion—all this, and yet—a fool!

And what of the thousands and tens of thousands of men

absorbed in business until they have no room for God, no time for prayer, no moments for meditation in the hushed silence of eternity? Fools!

What of the women, immersed in fashion, steeped in frivolity, the slaves of 'society,' the drudges of the froth of civilization? Very beautiful, very gay, many of them very winsome, but all—fools!

Of myself I dare not say that; but it stands as the verdict of the Eternal Wisdom, 'The fool hath said in his heart, No God.' And whoever is saying it, either *with* the lips or *in* the life, is thereby stamped for all the eternities a fool!

2. Let us think now of the second class—Fools in regard to knowledge.

'Fools despise wisdom and instruction;' there is another text from that Divine treasury of human experience—the Bible, and, like the previous one, it stands as a universal truth. 'How long will . . . fools hate knowledge?' asks the wise man. For ever, is the answer of Experience. It is not that they hate the wise, or hate the fruits of knowledge in others; not that they despise those who by wisdom open up the secrets of the universe for us. No; what they hate is the labour, the toil, the incessant application necessary to the attainment of knowledge, what they despise is the heavy, steep, rough road to wisdom. The pleasures of the senses are much stronger in their appeal than the pursuit of knowledge. It is easier to remain ignorant than to grow wise; and because it is easier, the majority choose it, but their choice makes them fools.

I was talking to a lady not long since about one of John

Ruskin's books, and she confessed to me that she did not read Ruskin much, because she found it so hard to understand him. Not that she *could not* understand, but because she found it *hard* to understand. Precisely; that is the spirit of the age. We like to have our thinking done for us, and take our scraps of knowledge as we take medicine—in homœopathic doses. The man who makes strong appeals upon our brain force, who harrows our reason, and makes us rub our brows, and literally dig out his meaning, we do not like that man. We want someone to analyze his work, bring his great thoughts down to little simple propositions, turn his grand, archaic, philosophic terms into vulgar English; then we say, 'Dear me, how interesting!'

There never was a time in the history of the world when knowledge was so accessible to universal man as it is now, and probably there never was a time when it was more universally despised. Think how that for a few shillings we can buy books that will give us a whole treasure-house of knowledge on almost every phenomenon of the universe. And yet how few avail themselves of them! Is it not a sorry proof that the wise man's dictum of the fools of his day is true of the fools of to-day—that where one scientific handbook, dealing with questions that affect life on every side, is sold, a thousand novels find buyers?

A great wise man writes a book on some of the laws of the universe—say astronomy, or geology, or mineralogy, or botany, or zoology; another man, not wise, but witty, smart, with an eye to those three almighty letters £ s. d., writes a novel dealing with the eternal sex question, a novel that a sensible reviewer does not hesitate to stamp as 'smutty.'

Which, think you, will have the larger circulation? I will tell you. The great wise man thinks himself fortunate if five hundred copies of his book are sold; the pot-boiling writer of the smutty novel advertises the fact that the first edition of his book consists of fifty thousand.

Surely, Carlyle, thou wert right—'Thirty million people, mostly fools.' 'Fools hate knowledge.'

I am accidentally thrown into the company of a young man, and, being interested in every type of human being, I try to find out all I can about him. I learn that he is one of that over-worked and under-paid class of men known as city clerks. His hours are from nine to four. 'Delightful!' say I: 'I wish mine were! Then you have a good bit of spare time?' 'Oh yes, moderate.' 'You live in the suburbs, I presume?' 'Yes.' 'How, then, do you spend your evenings?' 'I read mostly.' 'Excellent!'

I begin to think I shall like that young man, and so I try to learn further, and to see if we have anything in common. Perhaps we are interested in the same studies. 'Are you studying history, or languages, or any of the physical sciences?' I ask. 'No; I am a novel-reader.' 'What! Wholly a novel-reader? Can you tell me the name of yon glistening star? Can you tell me the habits and the laws of the life of the primrose? Can you speak any language but your own vulgar tongue? Do you know anything of the history of the formation of this earth? No! And yet you spend your evenings novel-reading!'

Give me a label. I am sorry to do it—he is smart, well dressed, gentlemanly—but God says it, and he must go to his own place, a place among the 'thirty millions, mostly fools!' I label him Fool. And if I were to label everyone like him, the army of labelled ones would be mightier in number than the soldiers of the Queen.

Nor is the folly confined to the male sex. I am perfectly astounded when I talk to women, taking them as a class, at their utter want of knowledge of everything outside the domestic and social sphere. I cannot get up anything approaching enthusiasm for the latest thing in bonnets, hats, mantles, and gowns; I admire them greatly, but I can't discuss them. I don't want to talk about things domestic. To discuss my neighbours bores me ineffably. And when I have said this, what is there left but the last novel, the play of the moment, or society's latest function? And all this with a universe of worlds wanting to tell us their secrets, with flowers nodding to us to be recognised and understood, with millions of treasure-houses holding their doors ajar that we may go in and explore. Oh, if you would only give the time you spend on novels, literary scraps, and sentimental rubbish, to some definite study, you would not only inform your own mind, and have a source of lasting satisfaction in yourself, but you would enrich the world with higher ideals, nobler aims, and purer methods of life. For 'as the woman is, so is the man.' 'How long, ye simple ones, will ye love simplicity . . . and fools hate knowledge?'

3. I come now to the third class of fools indicated in the Bible, that is, fools in regard to worldly possessions.

There are two characters depicted to us in our Lord's parables as great examples of this kind of fool—Dives and he who is known as the Rich Fool. Both *immensely* rich, yet the one crying in Hades piteously and in vain for a drop of water to cool his parched tongue; the other dying suddenly at the moment when he thought his happiness had begun. Now, wherein lay the foolishness of these men? Not certainly in the fact that they were rich. Our Blessed Lord never spoke of riches as things in themselves to be condemned or despised. What He did condemn was the miserable folly of storing riches, and not using them to right ends.

In describing the condition of the Rich Fool, He does not so much as hint that there was anything blameworthy. The man's ground brought forth plentifully: that showed him a good farmer, and hence a worker with God. When barns proved too small to hold the produce of his land he would pull them down and build greater: that showed him a prudent man. Why, then, did God hurl that awful anathema at him—'Thou fool'? Why? Because the man regarded his stored riches as things to be kept to minister to his own selfish greed. God intended them to be used for the world's common good. That is clear from what our Lord adds as a comment on the parable: 'For so,' says He, 'is everyone who layeth up treasure for himself, and is not rich towards God.'

Money is good, riches are good, treasure is good, when honestly gained and rightly used; but to store them for the pleasure of having them, and with the gluttonish intention of making them minister to the lusts of a sensual life, is wicked; and the man who so acts is a fool.

And yet what an immense proportion of the thirty millions are fools in this sense!

Listen to John Ruskin on this question. Speaking to the merchants of Bradford in a lecture, he asked them: 'What is it you want? Suppose you get millions of gold pieces, what would you do with them? and what do you want them for? If you do not want money as a mere instrument to noble ends; if you only want it to hoard it, to pile it up, and to die worth (what a ghastly phrase—" to die worth "!), say, half a million, why not save all your pains, and practise writing ciphers, and write as many as you want? Write ciphers for an hour every morning in a big book, and say every evening, I am worth all these noughts more than I was yesterday. Won't that do?' he asks.

If not, why not? Noughts in a ledger are quite as useful to you as gold pieces in a bank that you mean to leave there till you die. It is not what you have, but what you *use*, that makes you rich; it is not what you gain, but what you hide, that makes you a fool. And yet the reverence of the world is for fools. A man may be a positive ignoramus, unable to speak the Queen's English, a good bit of a brute in his private life, and yet if it is known that he has a huge fortune in the bank, the world bows down before him, as the Israelites did before another golden calf. He dies; men speak of him as the dead millionaire. God's epitaph on his tomb is, 'Thou fool!'

The genuine riches are the riches gained by doing good. Not in accumulating, but in devoting; not in storing, but in wisely spending, does true wisdom lie. There would have been no tormenting flame for Dives if he had done his duty with his riches; there would have been no condemnation for the other rich man if he had had higher ideals of the uses of wealth.

If you would escape the awful epitaph, written by God's own finger, be selfless with that which you gain. Care less for what you are going 'to die worth' than for what is the true worth of living: even to be rich towards God, and to lay up treasure in heaven. And thus

> '**Make** the heavenly period
> Perfect the earthen.'

THE END.

www.ingramcontent.com/pod-product-compliance
Lightning Source LLC
Chambersburg PA
CBHW020244170426
43202CB00008B/215